JAPAN
A Short History
New Edition

Coen Nishiumi

IBC Publishing

Contents

Chapter 5: The Meiji Period

Chapter 6: Path to World War II

Chapter 7: The Era of Global Partnership

1. Prehistoric Era

Where do the Japanese come from? That question is still looking for a definitive answer, but it is a common belief in Japan that the Japanese are homogeneous; that is, that they form one race and one culture. This view is partly based on the fact that Japan is surrounded by ocean and cut off from the rest of the world. Over time, however, it is true that Japan has had a good deal of interaction and exchange with the rest of the world.

Japan consists of four major islands and almost three thousand smaller islands. In prehistoric times, more than fifteen thousand years ago, Japan was geographically connected to the Asian continent. The bones of mammoths and many other animals similar to those found on the continent have been discovered in Japan.

It is uncertain when human beings first inhabited Japan. There is a widely accepted belief that people came from southern Asia and the Pacific about twenty thousand years ago. It is also thought that people came from the north.

More than two thousand prehistoric artifacts have been unearthed in Japan. Many more artifacts date from after circa 8,000 B.C. During this time, life was characterized by primitive villages of hunters and fishermen. The people of this time made clay pots decorated with cord markings.

Jomon pottery.

Yayoi pottery.

The Japanese word for these cord designs is *jomon*, which is also the name given to the period and to the people living in Japan at that time.

During the Jomon Period, the Japanese gradually imported farming skills from the rest of Asia. At the same time, in China, the Chinese writing system and many other technologies were developed and spread to other countries. The Japanese also adopted certain aspects of Chinese culture around the third century B.C.

The Yayoi Period is the next era, which is characterized by its distinctive pottery and clay figures. The name "Yayoi" derives from the archeological site near Tokyo where artifacts from the period were first uncovered. There were many important developments during this time, including the implementation of Chinese agricultural techniques. Rice fields were irrigated, and wooden, bronze, and iron tools were used throughout the country. Over time, the Yayoi people largely displaced the original Jomon inhabitants.

Clay figure.

Yayoi bronze bell.

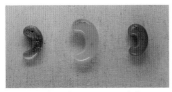

Fang-shaped accessories made from jade or agate.

2. Forming the Nation

While continental Asian influence was undeniably a pivotal element in the political and cultural history of ancient Japan, it is still unclear exactly how the Japanese were united as one nation. Modern Japanese may well be the descendants of continental Asian peoples that came to Japan in waves, one after the other. They had relatively sophisticated technologies that were influenced by the Chinese.

China was united around 221 B.C. when the Qin Dynasty and a new imperial government were established. Around the time of Jesus Christ, China greatly expanded its reach, becoming somewhat like the Roman Empire. One can easily imagine that there would be many interactions between an influential center of power such as China and the relatively weaker villages and tribes of Korea and Japan.

The Chinese impact stimulated some of these tribes to create more powerful political organizations. The very first recorded visit of a Japanese envoy to the Han court was in 57 A.D. However, the first movements toward creating nations in Korea and Japan probably did not begin until the third century.

During this time, the mysterious Japanese prophetess Himiko was mentioned in Chinese historical records. The

Yayoi bronze mirror thought to be used in religious rituals.

records say she was the queen of the Yamatai kingdom, which had contact with the court of the Wei Dynasty in China. The Japanese are described in these records as being law-abiding people who paid close attention to social hierarchies. They practiced agriculture and fishing, as well as spinning and weaving. The records further note that the rulers of the early Japanese were sometimes male and sometimes female.

Still today, archeologists argue about where Yamatai's capital was located. Some say it was in Kyushu, while others believe it was in the Yamato area, south of Kyoto. While the original capital may indeed have been in Kyushu, early legends suggest that, a century later, the predominant Yamato clan decided to move to the Yamato area where the first government was formed.

Reconstruction of Yayoi watch-tower at Yoshinogari site, Saga pref. Yoshinogari dates to between the third century B.C. and the third century A.D.

3. Yamato Years

Japan long regarded the emperor as being divine. Today, of course, the imperial system is more like the system of the United Kingdom. The emperor is seen as merely a symbol of the nation, and the imperial court has no political power.

The situation was different until the end of World War II. From the beginnings of their history until 1945 the Japanese followed and respected the same imperial tradition. The emperor had great influence on Japanese culture, although not always in politics, where the warrior class was often paramount.

A strong imperial government was first formed around the end of the third century A.D. It is referred to as the Yamato Imperial Court, because it was located in the region called Yamato. This region is south of Kyoto and extends to the center of the Kii Peninsula. Although it is not entirely clear how such a strong government came into being, it seems to have been forged through an intense power struggle.

This power struggle was related to political movements on the Korean Peninsula. According to Chinese histories of the time, the Japanese were asked to send troops to help support Paekche (Kudara in Japanese) during the battles between Korean kingdoms. Paekche is located in the southwest part of the Korean Peninsula. In the year 391, Japanese troops fought a major battle with Koguryo (Kokuri), the kingdom to the north.

This event suggests an intriguing possibility —namely, whether the Japanese imperial clan originated, in fact, in Korean peoples that invaded Japanese soil in earlier years. If this is true, it might be that the Japanese emperor sent troops to Korea to protect his own interests.

Keyhole-shaped burial mound for the Emperor Nintoku (fourth century), one of the biggest for its size in the world.

Or did the Japanese unite and marshal their forces with a view to conquering the Korean Peninsula. Many hypotheses are still heard today among archaeologists, anthropologists, and historians as to what actually happened and why.

Since the end of the fourth century, the Japanese would, from time to time, reveal their political and territorial interest in Korea. In 662 the Chinese navy effectively stifled that interest by defeating the Japanese navy and supporting Shilla (Shiragi), the kingdom in the southeast part of the Korean Peninsula.

This series of battles indicates that Japan was deeply involved with the Asian continent from the beginning of its recorded history. Japan did not, in fact, take its early identity from any domestic initiative. It took it from the consciousness of its connections with Korea and even China, which was also interested in influencing the Korean Peninsula.

In fact, when the Japanese imperial government was formed, thousands of Koreans and Chinese came to Japan, to be hired by the government and powerful local leaders and contribute to the country's development. In addition to technology, they also brought *kanji*, or Chinese characters, a sophisticated writing system that the Japanese adopted. Also, many Japanese emperors sent delegations to China to create economic, cultural, and political interactions with the Chinese government.

The power of the Yamato government can be seen in their *kofun*, or burial mounds. Between the third and fifth centuries, the imperial family and strong local leaders created huge *kofun* throughout Japan, most of which were centered in the Yamato region and surrounding areas. The most massive was that built in the fifth century for Emperor Nintoku. With a distinctive key-hole shape, it is one of the largest tombs in the world.

From the fifth century and into the sixth, Yamato emperors established their influence throughout Japan. The only areas they didn't influence were the northern part of Honshu and Hokkaido. These areas were considered almost separate nations with different tribes of people.

4. Arrival of Buddhism

Buddhism first came to Japan in the middle of the sixth century, principally through the medium of Chinese and Korean priests. Buddhism was not only a religion and a philosophy; it was also a distinctive, cosmopolitan civilization. The priests, who were the scholars and intellectuals of the time, brought valuable practical culture with them. This included medical technology and irrigation, along with their worldview.

Buddhist temples are everywhere in Japan today. One might think that Buddhism was an important part of Japanese culture from the very beginning of its history. But that is not the case. In fact, Buddhism could be considered the sixth-century symbol of internationalization.

After Siddhartha Gautama created this cosmopolitan religion, it took 1,000 years to reach Japan. During that time, Buddhism came in contact with other cultures and religions. For example, the expedition of Alexander the Great to Central Asia brought Greek culture into contact with Buddhism. Of course, with its establishment in India, Buddhism had considerable influences from ancient Indian civilization. Many other influences helped shape Buddhism as it gradually moved eastward through China, Southeast Asia, and Korea. Thus, when Buddhism finally arrived in Japan, it brought not only a distinctive religion but other benefits, including its cosmopolitan view of the world.

Daibutsu at the Asuka-dera.

However, Buddhism was very new to Japan and very different from its indigenous culture. Some people were concerned about its influence on Japanese life. They thought Buddhism might have a distrupting impact, much like the invasion of an alien civilization. Indeed, this concern created serious political conflict among the powerful clans of the imperial government. This struggle came to an end in 587 A.D., when the Soga clan, which supported Buddhism, defeated the opposing Mononobe clan.

During the era of the Soga clan's ascendancy, Buddhism was widely accepted under the auspices of the Yamato imperial government. Prince Shotoku established his leadership at this time as regent to the Empress Suiko. He began an official

Prince Shotoku (574–622) with his two sons.

diplomatic relationship with the Sui Dynasty of China and sent envoys called *kenzuishi*. This envoy system continued to the beginning of the tenth century. Through it, hundreds of students were sent to study in China.

Prince Shotoku is also known as the creator of Japan's first constitution, with its renowned seventeen articles. His era is called the Asuka Period and was named after the location of the government. The Asuka Period is associated with the earliest Buddhist culture in Japan. Horyu-ji temple, the oldest wooden structure in the world, was built during this time. Its architecture and sculptures reveal a great amount of influence from other countries.

After the death of Prince Shotoku in 622, a power struggle began between the Soga and rival clans. Eventually, in 645, Prince Nakano-oe (or Nakano-oe no Oji), who was supported by Nakatomi no Kamatari, assassinated Soga no Iruka, head of the Soga clan. This coup d'etat started a complete reformation of the imperial government, which was called the Taika Reform.

The new government consolidated its power based on the Chinese model. The main change was to implement effective tax management through a registry system. Prince Nakano-oe became Emperor Tenji in 668. Before leaving the throne in 672, he had established a new bureaucracy and legal system. The imperial government utilized Buddhist philosophy and religious power to stabilize the country.

5. Nara Period

When Yakushi-ji temple was built in Japan near the end of the seventh century, China was in the early stages of the Tang Dynasty. Tang China was one of the most prosperous empires in world history, its territory reaching as far as the eastern edges of the Middle East. In the Middle East, there was much exchange between eastern and western cultures. This was due in part to the fact that China's western neighbor at the time was the Saracen Empire, the influence of which reached as far as western Europe. In fact, China and the Saracens were the world's two leading civilizations, boasting the most advanced technology of the time.

The trade route between China and the Saracens was called the Silk Road. Countless merchants, monks, students, and soldiers traveled this road. It was the path along which the art of paper-making came to the West from China. This happened after the Saracen army defeated the Tang army in 751 A.D. Marco Polo was to travel along this route six hundred years later. The Silk Road stretched as far west as Italy and Spain and as far east as Japan.

Between Prince Shotoku's era and the beginning of the ninth century, Japan was greatly influenced by China and its cosmopolitan civilization. The imperial government established a law called the Taiho Constitution. This law covered legal matters, tax, social class, the military, and the political system.

When the Empress Gemmei decided to move the capital to Nara in 710, Japan already had a sophisticated government and legal system. When the city of Nara was designed, the grid pattern of Chang'an, the Tang Dynasty capital, served as a model. The era between 710 and 784 is called the Nara Period.

The Nara Period was an eminently active era. Numerous envoys were dispatched to the Tang court. Many students sent to study in China returned to Japan to play important governmental roles. Japan circulated its first currency during this time.

The Nara Period is also known as the era when Buddhism started to influence Japanese politics. Emperor Shomu believed that if Buddhism was revered, national crises such

Todai-ji temple, the iconic temple of the Nara Period with its gigantic statue of Buddha.

Yakushi-ji temple, erected around 680 A.D. in the suburbs of current Nara city.

as rebellions and natural disasters could be prevented. Thus, he ordered a huge statue of Buddha to be built in the capital. This statue can be seen today in Todai-ji temple in Nara. Todai-ji is also known for its treasure house, the Shoso-in, a repository of a variety of musical instruments, pottery, and decorative arts that came from China, India, and the Middle East.

Imperial support of Buddhism afforded Buddhist monks a position of power, and they began to exert influence on the central government. In the end this led to political turmoil after the death of Emperor Shomu. The first problem was the heavy taxes levied on farmers to build Todai-ji and the negative impact in had on their lives.

Nara was also the era in which Japan's first historical documents, *Kojiki* (Records of Ancient Matters) and *Nihonshoki* (The Chronicles of Japan), were published. *Kojiki* narrates the mythology of ancient Japan. *Nihonshoki* tells the history of the Yamato era. The most notable Nara publication was the *Man'yoshu* (Collection of Myriad Leaves), an anthology of poetry compiled sometime after 759. The Nara era came to an end in 784 when Emperor Kammu decided to move the capital to Nagaoka, in the suburbs of present-day Kyoto.

6. Era of Reconciliation between Shintoism and Buddhism

The Nagaoka capital was abandoned before it was even completed owing to political strife, to be relocated again to Heian-kyo in 794. Today Heian-kyo is known as Kyoto. The period of time from that date until 1192 is known as the Heian Period. Heian-kyo, like Nara, was modeled after the capital of the Tang Dynasty, Chang'an. The early part of the Heian Period was similar to the Nara Period, with a great deal of Asian influence. There were trade relationships with China, Korea, and Balhae (Bokkai in Japanese), a kingdom located in Manchuria and eastern Siberia.

At the beginning of the ninth century, the priests Saicho and Kukai returned from China and started two new Buddhist sects, the Tendai and Shingon, both of which became very influential. Their philosophical theories were steeped in complexity, and monks had to study and train for years to master them. Many temples were built deep in the mountains, where monks lived lives cut off from the mundane world.

Gradually, these new Buddhist sects mingled with the local Japanese religions and created a new set of religious practices. Traditionally, Japanese believed that *kami*, or spirits, were inherent in nature. Mountains, waterfalls, lakes,

Model of Heian-kyo.

The huge torii gate at the entrance to the funeral facilities where Kumano Shrine once stood.

stones and trees were respected as embodying those spirits. This belief developed over time and became ritualized. These rituals became the religion known as Shinto, or the "Way of the Gods."

Shinto is often seen as the religion of the imperial family. That is partly true. There are many Shinto shrines deeply related to the imperial family. A typical example is Ise Shrine, which was built in the early part of the Yamato era. However, every local region had its own beliefs in the spirits of nature. These local religions later erected shrines to show respect for their *kami*. In the late nineteenth century, these regional religions were officially unified as Shintoism.

During the ninth century, the new Buddhist sects began to adopt Shinto practices. For example, Buddhist monks began to show their respect for nature with various Shinto rites, such as purification. Through this process, Buddhism was eventually recognized as the national religion during the Heian Period.

Showing respect through rituals or established forms has persisted into modern Japan, including the Japanese business world. These practices can be seen, for example, when business cards are exchanged, or when a Shinto priest recites prayers at the construction site of a new building. It is also seen in the special way the stock exchange is closed at the end of every year. Such rituals and conventional acts are still thought to be quite important to doing business in Japan.

7. Era of *The Tale of Genji*

The adaptation of Shintoism by Buddhists was part of a process of "Japanizing" foreign culture. This has been a trend throughout Japan's history, and the Heian Period offers an excellent example. In China, the Tang Dynasty was collapsing and finally succumbed in 907. Civil war was followed by the emergence

Murasaki Shikibu.

of the Song Dynasty in 960. This led to a lapse in connections with China and gave Japan the leeway to absorb Chinese culture and transform it into something thoroughly Japanese. This process eventually helped Japan establish its own cultural identity.

One example of this process is how the Japanese adopted Chinese characters, making many of them simpler and creating their own writing system. The resultant system was a mixture of Chinese characters and the phonetic systems *hiragana* and *katakana*. Using this system, the Japanese created a rich variety of novels, poems and essays.

Perhaps the best known of these literary works is Lady Murasaki's *Genji Monogatari*, or "The Tale of Genji," which was brought to completion at the beginning of the eleventh century. This great love story is considered by many to be the world's first novel. Indeed, the Heian Period was a time of great literary creativity. Some of the best writing was done by women who were the daughters, wives, and mistresses of aristocrats. The world described in *The Tale of Genji* encompasses the life of the imperial court and its aristocratic inhabitants.

The principal political power in the Heian Period was the Fujiwara clan. They were the descendants of Nakatomi no Kamatari, who played an important role in the Taika Reform of 645. The Fujiwara clan held its power by two main strategies—economic and political. The clan controlled large areas of farmland throughout Japan. They also gained influence through marriages with the emperor's family. However, their extravagant lifestyle eventually created dissatisfaction in the imperial court. Indeed, while the Fujiwara clan was enjoying its prosperity, a new movement was looming in the rural areas.

In both the Nara and early part of the Heian Period, all land belonged to the nation. There was one important exception, however. Rural land that was newly cultivated could be privately owned. For this reason, the Fujiwara clan and powerful temples invested heavily in cultivating new land in the provinces. As a consequence, the imperial tax system that had been established with the Taiho Constitution gradually collapsed. In order to protect their private estates and to collect taxes from them, the Fujiwara and other powerful aristocrats and temples hired professional samurai, called *bushi*, to do their bidding. Around the middle of the tenth century, many of these warriors owed allegiance to two of the most powerful clans in the country, the Genji and Heike.

In 1086, after several military set-tos, the Fujiwara clan returned the political power it had gained in the imperial court to the imperial family. On the other hand, however, the economic and political situation worsened. The reason for this lies in the fact that the emperor was more or less subject to the same economic pressures as the Fujiwara clan. In fact, he also needed professional warriors to keep the government safe and stable. Thus it was that these powerful warrior clans began to transform the imperial court and aristocratic society.

The Tale of Genji, "Young Murasaki."   *The Tale of Genji, "His Perfumed Highness."*

8. The Genji and Heike

By the mid-twelfth century, samurai had begun to play a major role in Japanese politics. Two rival clans, the Genji and the Heike, battled for dominance between 1159 and 1185. Their struggle is often referred to as the Gempei War.

In the beginning, the Heike clan emerged preeminent under the leadership of Taira no Kiyomori. Later, it suffered a series of decisive defeats at the hands of the Genji. The Heike's struggles are described in the epic literary work *Heike Monogatari*, or *The Tale of Heike*. Nobody knows who wrote this lengthy narrative. Its lyrics were long sung by traveling monks to the accompaniment of a *biwa*, or Japanese lute.

After the fall of the Heike, the Genji commander Minamoto no Yoritomo was appointed shogun (supreme general or generalissimo) and became the effective leader of the country. Yoritomo established his military government, or shogunate, in Kamakura in 1192. This meant there were two seats of government in the country, causing considerable frustration at the imperial court in Kyoto. This frustration came to a head in the assassination of the third shogun, Minamoto no Sanetomo.

The instigator of the assassination was the family of Yoritomo's wife, the Hojo clan. After the success of their plot, the Hojo assumed leadership of the shogunate as regents acting on behalf of the shogun. Hoping to take advantage of political turmoil in Kamakura following Sanetomo's assassination, the imperial army launched an attack in 1221, but failed to overcome the shogunate forces.

Subsequently, although the emperor continued to be respected as the highest figure in Japanese society, executive powers were actually in the hands of the shogun. This system,

Minamoto no Yoritomo, the first leader (shogun) of a military government in Japanese history.

in various forms, lasted until 1868, when the Meiji Restoration ushered in a modern form of government.

Battle of Dan-no ura. The final stage of the Gempei War.

The establishment of a shogunate coincided with an important cultural shift in wider society. That is, a gradual transition from admiration of the gentleman and the scholar to a new respect for loyalty and honor among samurai. Bushido, "the code of the warrior," delineates the ideals of courage, duty, and self-sacrifice expected of a samurai. This way of thinking became deeply ingrained in Japanese psychology, and to this day it is evident in various aspects of Japanese society.

Tsurugaoka Hachiman Shrine, Kamakura.

9. Creation of People's Buddhism

During the Kamakura Period (1185–1333), many new Buddhist sects were established. Among the most important was Jodo-shu, or the Pure Land Sect. Jodo-shu originated in the tenth century as Jodo-kyo, became known as Jodo-shu under the priest Honen, and was further developed by the priest Shinran as Jodo Shinshu, or the New Pure Land Sect, in 1224.

The central tenet of Jodo Shinshu held that if people repeat the *nembutsu* chant ("I take refuge in Amida Buddha"), they will be saved after death because of the boundless mercy of Amida (Amitābha). In addition, Jodo Shinshu believed that this world is like an illusion, that nobody or nothing lasts forever, so just to believe and to utter the *nembutsu* meant salvation after death. Jodo Shinshu was quite popular because of its simple philosophy. It also responded to the needs of the era, when society was unstable because of war, disease, and poverty.

Nichiren-shu, another sect established in the thirteenth century, by the priest Nichiren, centered on recitation of the Hoke-kyo, or Lotus Sutra, a key Buddhist text. Nichiren was an exclusivist and criticized other religious sects that did not follow his beliefs and practices. After he warned Kamakura that there would be a national crisis, such as a foreign invasion, and Mongolia did in fact send troops to Japan soon thereafter, he also became widely known as a prophet. His activities were so zealous that he was prosecuted several times by the shogunate.

↑ *The internationally-known rock garden at Ryoan-ji temple was created in the late fifteenth century.*

← *The main gate of Kencho-ji temple is in the typical style of the Zen temples of the twelfth century.*

Nichiren (1222-1282), a Buddhist monk in Kamakura Period.

These new sects can be compared to dissenters against the Roman Catholic Church in medieval Europe, because they criticized traditional Buddhism for its great wealth, bureaucratic ways, corruption, and political influence. While traditional Buddhism and the shogunate saw these sects as threats, vast numbers of ordinary people accepted them as more intimate and easier to understand than established Buddhism, which required rigorous study and training. As a result, these new sects soon entered the mainstream of Japanese Buddhism.

Another important sect, Zen, was introduced to Japan from the Song Dynasty in China in the thirteenth century. Zen values the disciplines of meditation and physical training to overcome the troubles of daily life. Because of its stoic way of thought, Zen was widespread among the samurai class, which emphasized strict mental and physical discipline. Many Zen temples, which are particularly numerous in Kamakura and Kyoto, were built between the twelfth and fifteenth centuries and were supported by powerful warriors. They were not only beautiful for their architecture, sculpture, and painting, but also for their gardens. Gardens played a particularly important role as settings for meditation. Nanzen-ji, Ryoan-ji, and Daitoku-ji in Kyoto are the most important Zen temples featuring such beautiful gardens. In Kamakura, there are Kencho-ji and Engaku-ji, among others.

Even now Jodo-shu, Nichiren-shu and Zen are the three largest Buddhist sects in Japan.

10. Mongolian Invasion and the Fall of Kamakura

During the time when these new Buddhist sects were proliferating in Japan, China was experiencing a massive invasion from the north. First, the Manchurians invaded northern China and then toppled the Song Dynasty in the south. A second wave of invasions came from Mongolia, usurping Manchurian territory and establishing a new empire, the Yuan Dynasty, in northern China.

The Mongolian empire was vast, extending to the Middle East and even into Europe. After consolidating the Yuan Dynasty, Kublai Khan, the most powerful of the Yuan emperors, turned his eyes toward Japan. In his first attempt in 1274, he sent 30,000 Korean and Mongolian troops with advanced weapons using gunpowder. However, a typhoon forced their ships back and foiled their plans. Thereafter, the Yuan vanquished the Southern Song Dynasty and subjugated all of China.

Kublai Khan made another attempt in 1281 with 150,000 Korean, Mongolian, and Chinese soldiers, dispatched from Korea and southern China. This was the only invasion of Japanese soil prior to 1945, when Japan was occupied by the Allied nations after World War II.

How did the Japanese defend themselves? First, they were well prepared. After the first invasion attempt, they erected

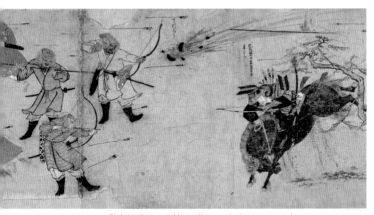

Fighting between Mongolians and a Japanese warrior.

Kublai Khan, the first Mongolian emperor, united China under his rule in the thirteenth century.

walls around Hakata Bay in northern Kyushu, which kept the invaders immobilized for fifty-four days on the seashore. Second, the Mongols were not used to fighting at sea and were harried by Japanese attacking in small boats. And third, yet another typhoon suddenly arose, this time destroying the Mongolian fleet.

Having been twice saved by timely typhoons, people looked upon them as miracles vouchsafed by the gods of Shinto and its doctrine of reverence for nature and nature's power. They referred to these two typhoons as *kamikaze*, or divine winds. This belief contributed to the Japanese notion of their own uniqueness—that is, that the Japanese were a divinely favored people—and was later used in militaristic propaganda in the years leading up to World War II.

After failing twice, the Mongols did not try again. However, the attempted invasions brought one noteworthy result in Europe. The Italian merchant Marco Polo, who served the Yuan Dynasty around this time, introduced Japan to the West as a land overflowing with gold and thus stimulated Europeans to travel to Asia. The Mongolian invasions also damaged the Kamakura shogunate economically and caused social unrest. Subsequently, no talented leaders arose who could resolve the economic and political problems inside the shogunate.

Finally, powerful supporters inside the shogunate decamped and joined the imperial court to oppose Kamakura. After several years of turbulence, the Nitta and Ashikaga, the two most powerful shogunate clans, decided to betray Kamakura. Thus, the Hojo clan, the actual power behind the shogunate, perished, and its government came to an end in 1333. Simultaneously, the imperial court in Kyoto established a new government under the leadership of Emperor Godaigo.

11. Era of Two Imperial Courts

When the Kamakura shogunate fell, the emperor's intent was to re-establish the authority of the imperial court as in ancient Japan. However, this attempt, known as the Kemmu Restoration, quickly failed, as it was incompatible with the reality of samurai society in the fourteenth century. The Ashikaga clan, supported by the samurai, finally wiped out the new government in Kyoto and created another imperial court with a branch family. Meanwhile, Emperor Godaigo escaped to Yoshino, south of Nara, and set up the so-called Southern Court in 1336.

At the same time, the imperial court in Kyoto appointed Ashikaga Takauji, head of the Ashikaga clan, as the new shogun. Thus, the Ashikaga shogunate was established in Kyoto and referred to as the Muromachi shogunate, named after the place where it was located.

This period of two imperial courts, with two emperors, is called the Southern and Northern Courts era, named after a similar period in Chinese history. The first thirty years presented a number of critical challenges to the Ashikaga shogunate. Perhaps the biggest challenge came from the Yamana clan, a former ally of Ashikaga Takauji, which changed its allegiance to the Southern Court. One Yamana leader, Kitabatake Chikafusa, was particularly zealous in the cause of re-establishing Godaigo as the legitimate emperor. His excellent strategy and guerrilla tactics occupied much of the Ashikaga shogunate's attention. Meanwhile, a quarrel between Takauji and his brother fomented internal conflict, further weakening

Emperor Godaigo.

Ashikaga Yoshimitsu.

the cause of the Northern Court.

The continual tumult and turmoil was finally brought under control around the time of the third Ashikaga shogun, Yoshimitsu. He had been appointed shogun in 1368 when he was only eleven years old. Over time, he demonstrated a deft political talent at managing the major samurai clans, eventually establishing an iron-clad dictatorship.

Ashikaga Takauji, the first shogun of the Muromachi (Ashikaga) shogunate.

Yoshimitsu persuaded the Southern Court to return to Kyoto in 1392 by agreeing to a compromise calling for imperial succession to alternate between the lines of the Southern and Northern Courts. He also persuaded the emperor to confer on him the highest rank at the imperial court. Later he reneged on his promise, ignoring the Godaigo line (it supplied no further emperors), but his power had been consolidated and the Ashikaga clan was preeminent.

Statue of Kusunoki Masashige, powerful supporter of the Southern Court.

12. From Prosperity to Chaos

After his political power was consolidated, Yoshimitsu became an avid supporter of new Zen temples in Kyoto and Kamakura. In Kyoto, he backed the construction of a series of large Zen temples, including Nanzen-ji, Daitoku-ji, Tenryu-ji, Myoshin-ji, and Tofuku-ji. He also constructed his famous villa, Kinkaku-ji, or the Temple of the Golden Pavilion, inside the Rokuon-ji temple grounds. Today this gold-foiled villa is one of the most popular tourist attractions in Kyoto. This era marked the height of a magnificent Buddhist culture, called Kitayama, or Northern Mountain, because Yoshimitsu's villa was located at the foot of the mountains north of Kyoto.

Toward the end of the fifteenth century, the Ashikaga shogunate fell into decline. One factor was the escalating internal power struggles, giving powerful clans a chance to assert themselves in governing the nation. Another was that, temples originally supported by the Ashikaga shogunate started to exercise their influence.

During the Muromachi (Ashikaga) era, local samurai clans, which were originally appointed as provincial governors by the Kamakura shogunate, extended their political power in their respective areas. The Ashikaga shogunate was meant to be the power center that united and controlled those clans. Ashikaga's internal conflicts, however, provided an opportunity for local clan lords to become independent. When the Onin War (1467–77) broke out, it inflicted fatal damage on the Ashikaga. Much of the fighting took place in Kyoto, and the city suffered irreparably. During these struggles,

Nanzen-ji temple.

Tofuku-ji temple.

↑ *Noh theater.*

← *Ashikaga Yoshimasa.*

Ashikaga Yoshimasa, the eighth Ashikaga shogun, retired to the eastern mountains of Kyoto, where he created the villa called Ginkaku-ji, or the Temple of the Silver Pavilion. In his villa he devoted himself to art and theater, having grown tired of politics and fighting. It was at this time, under Yoshimasa's patronage, that the Noh theater (masked drama combining dance, music, and chant) was developed by Kan'ami and his son Zeami.

In fact, many of Kyoto's temples are now located in the mountains and hills north and east of the city, as those areas were relatively safe from the ravages of the Onin War. During that war, the shogun came to be regarded as nothing more than a symbol of samurai hierarchy, while in the provinces local lords fought among themselves to expand their influence and territory. This marked the beginning of the Warring States Period.

Tenryu-ji temple.

13. The Warring States Period

Soon after the Ashikaga shogunate became politically ineffective in the late fifteenth century, major local lords created their own legal and political systems. They acted as though they were independent countries, and rural areas under their control began to flourish. In their major cities the markets were unrestricted and grew freely. Kyoto's sophisticated culture, and foreign culture as well, filtered down to the local level.

It was a time of diversity and opportunity. As the medieval system declined due to weakened central leadership, the old hierarchical system itself gradually changed. This trend can be seen in the politics of local lords. It became relatively common for lower-ranking samurai to usurp power from their nominal lords and set themselves up as lords themselves. With greater decentralization, economic and cultural activity throughout Japan took on new life.

This decentralization also resulted in the proliferation of provincial and castle towns. One of these new towns, called Sakai, located just south of Osaka, underwent rapid growth and eventually took on the guise of a "free city." It gained enough importance and power as a trading center that it was able to bargain as a corporate entity with the shogunate. Sakai also gained some freedom to administer its own laws, and at one time the shogunate even resorted to borrowing money from the city's merchants.

Trade with China increased greatly during this period, being centered in Sakai and nearby Hyogo, currently Kobe. One of the most important imports from China was copper money. Japan was not at this time minting its own coins, so expanding trade relied on Chinese coins for currency. Iron, textiles, drugs, books, and art were among the goods imported during this period. The trade with China was immensely profitable, since Japanese goods sold in the Chinese market for five to ten times their value at home. Popular exports included weapons such as swords and luxury

Uesugi Kenshin.

China-bound Japanese trading ship.

This coin, called an Eiraku-sen, was minted in Ming Dynasty China and used as currency in Japan.

items like lacquerware and fans.

During the first half of the sixteenth century, there were many hard-fought battles, and some powerful new lords aligned with much bigger powers. Among the most active warlords of this period were the lord of Shimazu in southern Kyushu, the lord of Mori in the Chugoku region, the lord of Takeda in central Honshu, the lord of Uesugi in Hokuriku, the lord of Hojo in Kanto, and the lord of Date in Tohoku.

Takeda Shingen.

Date Masamune.

14. The Advent of Western Culture

One of the most enriching aspects of this period was global exchange. The Protestant Reformation in sixteenth-century Europe fomented conflict and competition among European countries. In addition, the Ottoman Empire in Turkey expanded its influence into Europe, and European powers felt restraints on economic and cultural exchange between East and West. As a result, Catholic nations such as Portugal, Spain, and Italy, hoping to expand their religious influence beyond Europe, explored ocean routes to the East. China at this time had been united under the Ming Dynasty since around 1368. Ashikaga Yoshimitsu opened official trade relationships with the Ming in 1404.

In addition to official trade, there was also illegal trade. Japanese pirates, called Wokou (Wako in Japanese), were well-known in China from their plundering of its coastline. Moreover, many local lords in western and southern Japan, wealthy merchants, and some large temples sent private trade missions to Korea and China. The Ming Dynasty's prosperity also attracted Europeans and many of them settled in southern China. This was especially true after the discovery of an ocean route to Asia. Among the most numerous and influential of the Europeans in Asia were the Portuguese, who landed on the Japanese island of Tanegashima off southern Kyushu in 1543. They brought with them firearms and related technology.

Francisco Xavier (1506-62), a co-founder of the Society of Jesus, brought Christianity to Japan.

Folding screen depicting foreigners in Japan.

In 1549 the Portuguese also introduced Christianity when the Jesuit priest Francis Xavier arrived after preaching in other Asian countries. Many Japanese lords welcomed the new religion, some becoming sincere believers, while others were more interested in the trade and technological advantages that Christianity offered. The Jesuit Alessandro Valignano reported to Rome in 1582 that there were 150,000 Christian converts and two hundred churches in Japan. In the same year, a delegation of Japanese Christians of noble lineage was sent to visit the Pope and the king of Spain.

The Jesuit priests were particularly successful in Kyoto, forging relationships with many influential lords. The Buddhist authorities there, alarmed at Christianity's success, brought pressure on the government to have these priests expelled. These priests retreated to Sakai, but their message was not as successful with the city's merchant population.

Detail of screen depicting foreigners in Japan.

15. Reunification

This encounter with Western culture took place at a time when the embattled country was moving toward unification. Around 1550, the country was still divided, with the major warlords having gradually expanded their territory and absorbed the jurisdictions of weaker domains. In 1573, after a series of battles, Oda Nobunaga, the lord of Owari (currently western Aichi Prefecture), sent his armies into Kyoto to topple the Ashikaga shogunate. Nobunaga succeeded and expelled Ashikaga Yoshiaki, the fifteenth Ashikaga shogun, from the capital. This ended the Muromachi shogunate and the Ashikaga line, as Nobunaga did not choose a successor for Yoshiaki. Neither did Nobunaga take the title of shogun for himself, preferring to support the imperial line while maintaining military hegemony.

Nobunaga is one of the most popular figures in Japanese history. He was the son of a minor lord but expanded his territory rapidly. He was a genius at military strategy and an aggressive leader. He welcomed Western influence and used it to enrich his territory. He valued the power of firearms and used them effectively when he and his ally, Tokugawa Ieyasu, defeated the Takeda clan, a powerful rival, in 1575.

Nobunaga then relocated his headquarters to Azuchi, on the shore of Lake Biwa near Kyoto, and started the process of reunification. Azuchi had an international atmosphere, with several European missionaries residing there. The Azuchi Castle was known even in Rome for its magnificence. To reunify the country, Nobunaga didn't hesitate to clash with Buddhist authorities, who were influential not only in religious affairs but in political matters as well.

Next Nobunaga began the process of subjugating the outlying regions. However, while the majority of his troops were engaged

Akechi Mitsuhide, the general who betrayed and killed Oda Nobunaga.

Oda Nobunaga.

Azuchi Castle, destroyed immediately after the death of
Oda Nobunaga in 1582.

in assailing the powerful Mori of western Honshu, he was betrayed by one of his own generals, Akechi Mitsuhide. While Nobunaga was passing through Kyoto in 1582, Akechi took him by surprise in a temple called Honno-ji. To avoid capture, Nobunaga committed suicide, his body consumed in the flames of the burning temple.

Folding screen depicting Battle of Nagashino.

16. Toyotomi Hideyoshi and His Era

The general who fulfilled Nobunaga's dream of uniting the country was Toyotomi Hideyoshi. He had been promoted by Nobunaga from the lowest samurai rank to become one of his top generals. At the time of Nobunaga's death, Hideyoshi was leading the assault against the Mori. Receiving word of Nobunaga's death, he quickly concluded a peace treaty with the Mori and rushed back to Kyoto to avenge Nobunaga's death by squelching Akechi. He then proceeded to bring down his remaining rivals, and in 1590 his (and Nobunaga's) dream was realized with the fall of the Hojo.

Toyotomi Hideyoshi's government was different from the former military governments in that he was considered simply as the highest-ranking lord. In other words, his authority did not come from a centralized government supported by locally appointed governors, each with his own jurisdiction and military system. He won their respect as a brilliant general and as the most powerful person in the land.

In that capacity, Hideyoshi reformed the system of weights and measures, conducted land surveys, and created a new tax system. Also, he strictly enforced class stratification and prohibited non-samurai from possessing weapons. His headquarters was established in Osaka, where he built Osaka Castle. He also had luxurious villas in Kyoto, from which he exercised control over the temples and imperial court.

↑ *Jurakudai. This gorgeous palace was used by Toyotomi Hideyoshi for both official business and as a private residence.*

← *Osaka Castle, originally erected by Toyotomi Hideyoshi in 1583.*

Sen no Rikyu, tea ceremony master active in the sixteenth century. He served as an advisor to Toyotomi Hideyoshi.

Toyotomi Hideyoshi, the dictator who united Japan after 100 years of civil war.

The era of Nobunaga and Hideyoshi is called Azuchi-Momoyama, a period when certain art forms achieved their highest expression. Many paintings were created on the walls and sliding doors of castles, temples, and villas, including works by the Kano school of painters, the most influential of the time. The tea ceremony was refined by Sen no Rikyu, the famous merchant and tea master serving under Hideyoshi.

Painting and the tea ceremony were integrated into the lifestyles of the noble and military classes. Many merchants and artists, on the other hand, appreciated exotic Western culture. The city of Sakai, known as a free international trading city, was governed by the merchants themselves until Nobunaga came to power. Ironically, during the internecine Warring States Period, the Japanese economy and lifestyle flourished, thanks to the investment of powerful local lords. When Nobunaga and Hideyoshi expanded their territory, they also inherited the benefits of those investments and were able to create a strong financial foundation.

But Hideyoshi's political career was not always successful. He tried twice to invade Korea, with an eye to conquering the Chinese Ming Dynasty. His first attempt was in 1592, when he dispatched 150,000 soldiers to the Korean Peninsula. Although they captured Seoul and Pyongyang, they were forced to withdraw by a guerrilla-style counterattack supported by Chinese troops and the Korean navy. Hideyoshi's second attempt was aborted due to his death in 1598. These failed incursions are sometimes mentioned in connection with the Japanese annexation of Korea in 1910.

17. Creation of the Tokugawa Shogunate

When Hideyoshi was on his deathbed, and his son Hideyori was still a small child. Hideyoshi appointed five regents to look after Hideyori until he was old enough to take the reins of leadership. The regent with the strongest influence was Tokugawa Ieyasu, lord of the Kanto plain in central Honshu. He was born in Mikawa, east of Nagoya, the son of a minor lord. When Oda Nobunaga began his push to unite the country under one leader, Ieyasu supported Nobunaga's ambition.

After Nobunaga's assassination, Ieyasu assumed a position of power second only to Hideyoshi. To acknowledge this, Hideyoshi granted Ieyasu the Kanto provinces of the Hojo clan, which he had taken in 1590. This move was beneficial to Hideyoshi because it moved Ieyasu further from the capital, reducing any threat to Hideyoshi's supremacy. However, Kanto was already well developed as an agricultural and industrial region, and it gave Ieyasu the freedom and means to develop his own power base.

Although Ieyasu did not oppose Hideyoshi's leadership, he had become quite influential and ambitious by the time

↑ Ishida Mitsunari, a general and former senior bureaucrat serving Toyotomi Hideyoshi. He was executed by Tokugawa Ieyasu after the battle of Sekigahara.

← Battle of Sekigahara monument.

Donjon of Osaka Castle.

Tokugawa Ieyasu, the first shogun of the Tokugawa shogunate.

of Hideyoshi's death. Ishida Mitsunari, the top bureaucrat in Hideyoshi's government, sensed the threat posed by Ieyasu and actively opposed him.

The two forces finally clashed in 1600 in the famous Battle of Sekigahara, between Nagoya and Kyoto, with Ieyasu defeating Mitsunari and his allies. After executing Mitsunari, Ieyasu consolidated his headquarters in Edo (current Tokyo). In 1603, the emperor appointed Ieyasu shogun. His position became unassailable in 1615 with the destruction of Osaka Castle, the last Toyotomi stronghold, which resulted in the suicide of Toyotomi Hideyori, Hideyoshi's son.

Many of the events at the turn of the seventeenth century provided the background for the best-selling novel *Shogun*, written by James Clavell. This series of incidents, from Nobunaga's rise to the demise of Hideyori in 1615, has been fictionalized by many Japanese novelists. The story also provides material for many a popular historical drama on Japanese television.

The Tokugawa shogunate lasted until 1868, when the emperor was restored to power and Japan started to modernize under the new Meiji government.

18. The Founding of the Tokugawa Shogunate

The most important task for Ieyasu and his successors was to create a solid political foundation. Based on their experience of civil war during the Warring States Period, they set out to establish a strong centralized government with all local lords under its authority. The lords who had been Tokugawa loyalists before the Battle of Sekigahara were appointed to high offices and granted many privileges. Other lords were relocated to rural areas, safely removed from the seat of power and carefully watched as potential sources of trouble.

Ieyasu built a massive castle and essentially a whole city from scratch in Edo, originally a fishing village, as the administrative center of the Tokugawa shogunate. He appointed his closest relatives as the lords of Wakayama (south of Osaka), Owari (Nagoya) and Mito (north of Edo) to oversee and protect those strategic areas. Unfortunately, the city of Edo (later Tokyo) and the castle itself have been destroyed more than once by fires, including the firebombing during World War II. The site of the original Edo Castle is the location of the current Imperial Palace.

The shogun also established a representative office in Kyoto to keep an eye on the activities of the imperial court, even though, in theory, the emperor was regarded as a

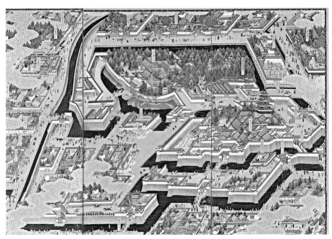

Seventeenth-century painting of Edo Castle.

Fushimi-yagura keep, Edo Castle (now Imperial Palace).

Moat, Edo Castle (now Imperial Palace).

divinity. As part of its authoritarian strategy, the Tokugawa shogunate owned approximately 25% of available land in Japan, dispersing the rest of it among the lords. These feudal domains were called *han*.

To create social stability, Ieyasu also tightened class structure along Confucianist lines. He divided the nation into four classes, with samu-

Bridge, Edo Castle (now Imperial Palace).

rai being the highest, then farmers, craftsmen, and merchants as the lowest. All manner of social activities, such as inter-marriage between classes, the changing of jobs, movement from one class to another, or even relocating were either prohibited or strictly controlled. This was accomplished by means of a detailed registration system and enforced by the

police. The shogun also strengthened the rule of group accountability—in other words, if a crime was committed, not only the perpetrator but also his or her family and sometimes even neighbors were prosecuted.

Sakurada Gate, Edo Castle (now Imperial Palace).

19. Closing the Nation

Overall, Tokugawa strategy had a huge impact on subsequent Japanese history. While Confucianism was known in Japan from the late Yamato Period, the Tokugawa rulers adopted its Neo-Confucian form to bolster the feudal social system. It was accepted rapidly by samurai society to undergird basic morality and provide models of behavior. In fact, Neo-Confucianism became an essential tool in establishing and maintaining social stability.

In particular, the sense of class, of hierarchy, of centralized government and bureaucracy, and of group-oriented behavior still remain as important structural and social values in Japan, distinguishing it from the more individualistic West. As a case in point, even now, whether in public affairs or private business, if a subordinate makes a serious mistake or commits a crime, his or her boss is considered to be responsible, too.

The most profound influence on modern Japanese mentality stems from the period of Japan's isolation from the rest of the world. The Tokugawa shogunate closed Japan's door to foreign countries in 1639, except for Dutch, Chinese, and Korean envoys. Even they were restricted to the small artificial island called Dejima in Nagasaki. This policy was inspired by the shogunate's concern over the territorial ambitions of Western nations. In addition, with Christianity's rapid growth, the shogunate feared that Christianity was the advance guard of a Western plot to colonize Japan.

By the beginning of the seventeenth century, the Dutch and British had begun to expand their trading activities in Asia. The Spanish and Portuguese had opened headquarters in Manila and Macao, respectively, to promote trade and religious relationships with Asians. Both countries had a big presence in Japan. The Dutch and British, however, took a different approach from their Catholic rivals, because they were interested solely in trade, not in missionary work. They persuaded the Tokugawa government to evict their Catholic rivals from the country. In the end, however, the British found Japan unprofitable and closed their trading post, located in Hirado in western Kyushu, in 1623.

The shogunate was unrelenting in its prohibition of

Dutch trader watching an incoming Dutch ship at Dejima.

Christianity. Countless Japanese converts faced martyrdom unless they recanted. The persecutions of Christians came to a dramatic climax in 1637, when Christian followers and farmers, suffering under a heavy tax burden, rebelled in Shimabara, near Nagasaki. This rebellion lasted about six months, and the shogunate dispatched over a hundred thousand soldiers to quell it.

After the rebellion, the shogunate intensified persecution and took a stronger stand against its Catholic trading partners. The Portuguese were ejected in 1639, and all Japanese living abroad were prohibited from returning home. During the first two decades of the seventeenth century, many Japanese sailed to Southeast Asia to create Japanese settlements and conduct trade with local and European merchants. Some lords, like Date of Sendai, sent envoys to the West. All such activities were strictly prohibited when the seclusion policy was promulgated in 1639. This policy continued until 1854, when the shogunate opened Japan's door under the pressure of American Commodore Matthew Perry and his black-hulled ships.

The most obvious benefit of the seclusion policy was the stability of the Tokugawa political and social institutions for more than two hundred years. Its drawback, however, was also far-reaching: industrially, Japan fell so far behind Western countries that it was almost impossible to catch up. Japan paid the price for this in the latter half of the nineteenth and in the twentieth century. Even more profound, this long seclusion gave the Japanese a complex sense of their own uniqueness—that they were a homogeneous island race different from all other peoples. This conviction persists in Japan today and is often cited as a reason for the Japanese inability to communicate globally.

20. The Period of Kabuki and Ukiyo-e

Under the seclusion policy and stable Tokugawa rule, Japan enjoyed domestic prosperity. Cities prospered and the merchant class developed a money-based economy. Around the beginning of the eighteenth century, more than one million people lived in Edo, making it the world's most populous city.

Supported by wealthy merchants and a vigorous economy, the arts reached unprecedented heights. Kabuki (grand, stylized, actor-centered drama) emerged to become a sophisticated performing art around the end of the seventeenth century. To celebrate Kabuki actors, city life, and the beauties of nature, woodblock brochures were widely circulated and became recognized as an art form called *ukiyo-e*. In the late nineteenth century, these prints had a profound impact on French impressionists.

With the invention of color woodblock printing in 1765 by Suzuki Harunobu, *ukiyo-e* made further advances as a commercial art. Kitagawa Utamaro, Katsushika Hokusai, and Toshusai Sharaku were among the most popular artists in the eighteenth and early nineteenth centuries. Book publishing was also quite active. Love stories and tragic tales with samurai heroes were widely circulated and adapted for Kabuki and the Bunraku puppet theater.

Edo period cultural activity had two peaks. The first began toward the end of the seventeenth century during the years of the fifth Tokugawa shogun, Tsunayoshi, and was called the Genroku era. It was a time of relative prosperity. Thanks to

Kabuki actors depicted in an ukiyo-e by Utagawa Kunisada.

the Pax Tokugawa, the martial skills of the samurai became less and less in demand. Many samurai took jobs as civil servants and came to prefer a relatively more extravagant lifestyle compared to the traditional warrior. This trend coincided with the burgeoning middle-class life of Edo. The Genroku era also saw the emergence of *haiku*, the seventeen-syllable poem. Matsuo Basho is well-known as the master of this poetic form.

Matsuo Basho.

The second cultural peak in the Edo Period occurred in the late eighteenth century, the Bunka-Bunsei era. Cultural activity thrived not only in Edo but also in Kansai (the area including Osaka and Kyoto.) For example, the playwright Chikamatsu Monzaemon adapted many famous stories for Bunraku and Kabuki in the Kansai area. It was also around this time that Western ships began to appear along the coasts to knock on the door of insular Japan. This eventually stimulated some scholars to travel to Nagasaki, where they could study Western culture through the medium of Dutch.

↑ *"Beauty looking back," by Hishikawa Moronobu.*

← *"Woman wiping Perspiration," by Kitagawa Utamaro.*

21. Decline of the Feudal System

Around the latter part of the eighteenth century, the social system created by the Tokugawa started to show signs of decay, particularly in the economy. Big cities were already operating on a currency-based system, while domain lords were receiving taxes in the form of rice grown by their vassals. Samurai salaries were also paid in rice. As a result, the samurai needed to exchange rice for money in order to survive. In fact, it was becoming quite common for city merchants to finance both lords and their samurai, who eventually became indebted to the merchants, who were ironically considered the lowest social class in the Tokugawa feudal system.

Rural lords shouldered additional burdens imposed by the shogunate. One of these was the *sankin kotai*, which required all lords, ostensibly for security reasons, to reside in Edo every other year. Traveling to Edo and back to their home province each year was exorbitantly expensive. Adding to this expense was the cost of maintaining two residences, one in Edo and the other in their home province or *han*.

Many lords tried to improve their financial situation through various means. For example, the Satsuma *han*, now Kagoshima prefecture, secretly conducted foreign trade through Okinawa. On the other hand, many lords simply failed, faced with rebellious farmers who protested against heavy taxes. In fact, many samurai became jobless or even homeless as a result of Tokugawa policy.

Ukiyo-e of Nihonbashi from The Fifty-three Stations of the Tokaido. While declining the feudal system, the merchant town were prospered.

The peasant farmers were abused and neglected as a class throughout the Tokugawa Period. They were allowed to keep just enough of their harvests to stay alive until the next year—the rest of the produce was taken as tax. If this were not enough, peasants were plagued by famine throughout this era. The three famines of 1732, 1783, and 1833 in particular caused intense suffering. As a result, it is no wonder that peasant uprisings and rebellions were not uncommon.

From the very beginning of the Tokugawa era, the shogunate sensed potential problems with those lords who swore allegiance to the Tokugawa only after the Battle of Sekigahara, and made their lives particularly difficult. In the end, many of these lords were stripped of their territory, leaving the thousands of samurai who served them without a livelihood. Such jobless samurai were called *ronin*, and they were ubiquitous. For the samurai, who occupied the highest social rank, to be in dire financial straits created a basic contradiction in Tokugawa society. The growing, powerful merchant class, large numbers of unemployed samurai, and continuous peasant rebellions created major internal anomalies for the Tokugawa rulers. This contradiction was compounded by another challenge: the appearance of foreign warships.

Matsudaira Sadanobu (1759-1829), famous for his financial, Kansei no Kaikaku, for Tokugawa Shogunate.

Tokugawa Yoshimune (1684-1751), the eighth shogun of the Tokugawa shogunate, undertook the big reform, Kyoho no Kaikaku, to save the financial crisis in late Edo.

22. Opening of the Nation and the Fall of the Tokugawa

In the eighteenth century, a number of foreign ships appeared in Japanese waters and attempted to instigate trade relations. But the shogunate stubbornly adhered to seclusion. However, when four U.S. frigates commanded by Commodore Matthew Perry arrived in Uraga Bay near Edo in 1853, the shogunate suddenly realized that it had been sleeping while the world passed them by.

Commodore Matthew Perry.

Four huge warships with advanced weaponry were quite enough to convince the shogunate to modify its policies. After lengthy negotiations, the Tokugawa leaders finally decided to open the country's doors in 1854. They allowed foreign access to several ports and started trade relationships, first with the United States and then with Russia, France, England, and the Netherlands.

This policy reversal was condemned by many Japanese nationalists, who believed that a decision of this magnitude should not be made without consulting the imperial court. They thought the emperor should be respected as Japan's supreme ruler, even though actual administrative power was still in the hands of the shogunate. Many samurai and even some lords held nationalist views and strongly urged the shogunate to resist "barbarian pressure."

The shogunate was fully aware that Western countries were colonizing Asian lands by means of their advanced military power and technology, and consequently it strove to suppress those opposed to its shift in policy. Thus, the nation was divided into two camps: those who opposed the shogunate's new foreign policy and those who supported it. Kyoto, where the imperial court was located, became the center of this struggle for power.

Perry's "Black Ships."

In terms of political influence, Satsuma (now Kagoshima prefecture, located in southern Kyushu) and Choshu (now Yamaguchi prefecture, located in western Honshu) had become the most influential domains. In the not-too-distant future Satsuma and Choshu would successfully promote talented young samurai into influential positions

The last Tokugawa shogun, Tokugawa Yoshinobu.

in the new Meiji government. These were the new leaders who would launch Japan on its modern trajectory. Initially, however, the two domains tried to remove foreign influence from Japan and even engaged the Western powers in battle. When the Western navies successfully counterattacked, they learned the necessity of developing advanced military power and technology.

Subsequently, Satsuma and Choshu led the effort to overthrow the old regime. After a series of battles, assassinations, and other tumultuous events, these two domains joined hands in 1866 to create an allied front against the Tokugawa, secretly supported by the imperial court. The coordinator of this alliance was Sakamoto Ryoma of Tosa (now Kochi prefecture in southern Shikoku), who was unfortunately assassinated after this secret agreement was made. The shogun was too weak economically and militarily to withstand the new movement.

Under immense pressure, Tokugawa Yoshinobu, the last shogun, resigned in 1867. At that point, the anti-Tokugawa forces attempted to establish a new government under the aegis of the imperial court. But Yoshinobu did not give up without a fight. After resigning, he concentrated his forces at Osaka Castle to oppose the anti-Tokugawa alliance led by Saigo Takamori, one of the distinguished new leaders from Satsuma. By 1868, Saigo had defeated the Tokugawa forces in the Kyoto suburbs of Toba and Fushimi. After escaping to Edo, Yoshinobu surrendered, bringing the feudal era to an end.

23. Meiji Restoration

The year 1868 is one of the most important in modern Japanese history. It was the year Japan officially set out to become a modern state. The new imperial government had swept away nearly all opposition forces still loyal to the Tokugawa shogunate. But as Tokugawa Yoshinobu surrendered, some lords persistently tried to fight back. A series of battles between the new government and the Tokugawa supporters ensued, which is collectively referred to as the Boshin War. The most famous battle took place in Aizu-Wakamatsu in Tohoku, where many samurai were killed and wounded. By April 1869, the last of the Tokugawa supporters was defeated in Hakodate, Hokkaido.

The new government decided to move the imperial court from Kyoto to Edo, which was renamed Tokyo (Eastern Capital). The task of the new government was obvious: to transform Japan into an advanced nation with a strong military and a robust industrial base. When the Emperor Komei died in 1866, the Emperor Meiji officially succeeded to the throne in September 1867. This is known as the Meiji Restoration.

Emperor Meiji.

A stable government was needed for both domestic and international reasons. To avoid the fate of many other Asian nations, which had been

Toshimichi Okubo.

Takamori Saigo.

During the Bosin War, samurai of the Choshu clan fought against Aizu Samurai.

In 1872, the first steam train between Shinbashi and Yokohama was opened.

colonized by Western powers, Japan's new leaders needed to create modern technology, military power, and administrative systems. Domestically, social class distinctions and samurai privileges were abolished under the leadership of Takayoshi Kido, Toshimichi Okubo, Tomomi Iwakura, the previously mention Takamori Saigo, and others.

The government began to conscript soldiers from among ordinary citizens. To create centralized authority, it abolished the old feudal domains and introduced a system of prefectures with governors appointed by Tokyo. The old financial system was converted to a modern banking and monetary system. New tax and legal policies were integrated under the central government. Railroads, telecommunications, and postal systems were established. The first rail service opened in 1872 between Tokyo and Yokohama. All these were important steps toward realizing the government's mission to overtake the West and protect the nation and its interests.

In end result, the encounter with the West caused Japan to gain a better sense of its own identity. Before the Meiji Restoration, Japan had been isolated for more than 230 years—a period during which it had developed a distinctive set of values and ethics. Now Japan was open to the world and had to adapt. The new leadership began its reforms by importing foreign technology with its attendant values and worldview. The mixture of the new with the traditional provided Japan with an opportunity to move forward. In retrospect, the Meiji Period also marked the starting point down the road to World War II, the result of a crucible of fate and opportunity that produced nationalism.

24. From the Seinan War to the Promulgation of the Meiji Constitution

To forge a modern nation, the Meiji government needed to overcome several challenges. The most important was to assuage the frustration of former samurai who had lost their privileges. Many of them tried to foment rebellion against the government. The Seinan War in 1877 was their most serious effort. It was sparked when Takamori Saigo, one of the heroes of the Meiji Restoration, left the government over stark political differences. His followers and many frustrated samurai pressed Saigo to rebel. His private army eventually numbered more than thirty thousand. Their rebellion started in Kagoshima (formerly Satsuma, Saigo's homeland) and spread throughout the southern part of Kyushu. However, within several months Saigo was overwhelmed by the powerful modern army dispatched from Tokyo, and he committed suicide in Kagoshima.

After the Seinan War, discontented samurai continued their protests with their voices instead of weapons. They asked the government to listen to their demands. They criticized it for not introducing representative democracy such as found in Western nations.

The Meiji government, however, considered such protests dangerous, embodying the seeds of further discontent. The government's aim was to create modern administrative, judicial and legislative powers under the authority of the

Battle of Tabaruzaka in the Seinan War.

Meiji Constitution promulgation.

emperor. After extensive internal confusion and argument, they finally installed a parliamentary system in 1889 with a constitution modeled after Germany's. The first imperial parliament, called the Diet, was opened the next year. The cabinet had already been created in 1885, with Hirobumi Ito appointed as the first prime minister.

In several respects, this parliamentary system was not completely democratic. Suffrage was granted only to tax-paying males. The upper house of the Diet was made up exclusively of aristocrats, the emperor's relatives, and individuals appointed by the emperor. The constitution made the Diet responsible solely to the emperor, who was considered the supreme authority. As it had done with the constitution, the government followed a European model—France—for its criminal and civil law.

Around the same time, the economy began to heat up, and manufacturing hit new heights. Particularly vigorous were the textile and shipping industries. However, these successes were largely due to strong governmental support of the wealthy privileged classes. Almost all ordinary citizens and farmers remained poor. As a result, during the tortuous attempts to create a parliamentary system, socialist movements gained momentum. The government first tried to deal with such recalcitrant elements by oppression and later by shifting attention to foreign wars and invasion.

25. Way to the Russo-Japanese War

The nineteenth century was the era of imperialism. England, France, Germany, Russia, the Netherlands, and later the United States were the major players in occupying foreign territory and creating spheres of influence in Asian and African nations. These Western nations concluded unequal treaties with Japan, curtailing its sovereignty. From the very beginning of the Meiji Period, the government's main task was to rectify these unfair conditions. Balance was not completely restored until Japan was recognized as a global military power.

Japan viewed Russia as its most serious threat because of its geographical proximity. Accordingly, it turned its attention first to the Korean Peninsula, for even though Korea was considered a tributary of the Qing Dynasty, the Japanese believed that strong influence in Korea would be the best way to protect Japanese interests from Russia. Thus, Japan demanded that Korea open its ports to trade, and then imposed its own unequal treaty. Finally, after manipulating Korea's internal politics, Japan forced it to accept a Japanese military presence. These activities provoked an eight-month war with China, which the Westernized Japanese military easily won.

In the Treaty of Shimonoseki of 1895 China ceded Taiwan, various other islands, and the Liao-dong Peninsula to Japan, and agreed to pay a war indemnity. However, Western nations, with their respective spheres of influence and assets in China, saw the Japanese victory as a threat. Eventually, Russia, Germany, and France demanded the restoration of the Liao-dong Peninsula to the Qing Dynasty. Japan reluctantly conceded to this demand, feeling it was too dangerous to have hostile relations with these three Western powers.

Still, the Japanese government used this unjustified international pressure to turn Japanese public opinion toward nationalism. They invested in the military and ramped up industrialization, and they continued their attempts to exercise influence in Korea.

The international power struggle in East Asia in the late nineteenth century involved nearly all the major Western countries seeking broader economic opportunities in China.

When the British clearly grasped Japan's concern about Russia's pressure, they opted to support Japan in order to defuse Russian territorial ambitions. Japan and England became allied in 1902, making official their common interest against Russia. The United States also supported Japan, because, following their annexation of the Philippines after the Spanish-American War in 1898, they wanted to establish an economic presence in Manchuria. France and Germany, on the other hand, were British rivals and therefore supported Russia.

Given these difficult and complex relationships, Japan and Russia faced formidable obstacles in establishing their interests in Manchuria and the Korean Peninsula. Japan finally declared war on Russia in February 1904, after ten years of preparation. This war posed great risks for Meiji Japan, as Russia was one of the reigning superpowers with vast territories, technology, and military might. While Japan clashed with the Russian army and navy in a number of bloody battles and exhausted its economic resources in the process, its efforts were heavily financed by England and the United States. At the same time, the Russian government feared that if they continued the war and debilitated their military and economy, the growing revolutionary movement in Russia would gain further momentum.

American president Theodore Roosevelt offered to mediate a peace treaty. Delegations from Japan and Russia met in the United States at Portsmouth, New Hampshire, to negotiate. Japan was awarded southern Sakhalin and ownership of the South Manchuria Railway. Thus, the Russo-Japanese War came to an end in 1905, after costing huge sums of money and the loss of many lives on both sides.

Russian Crusier Varyag in Chemulpo Bay during Russo-Japanese War.

26. Annexation of Korea

Japan and Russia fought their war mainly in China. It was the fate of Asia that Western powers and the new player, Imperial Japan, used Asia as their chessboard. There were people who opposed war in both Japan and Russia. In Japan, Socialists and Christian activists played an important antiwar role. The Christian philosopher Kanzo Uchimura and the Socialist activist Shusui Kotoku were the most well-known figures to speak out against imperialism.

Hirobumi Ito, a preeminent Japanese political leader and the first prime minister in Japanese history.

However, the vast majority of Japanese were exhilarated over Japan's triumph but also disappointed that it did not gain as much from the war as expected. The negotiations in Portsmouth were challenging for the Japanese side, since the Russians knew Japan had exhausted its resources and couldn't afford to continue the war. To counter the Japanese disappointment, to elicit respect for Japan among the Western powers, and to recover economic stability and national security, Japanese leaders like Hirobumi Ito believed that the annexation of Korea was indispensable.

When the war against Russia ended, Korea was completely under Japanese control. Korea protested to the international community, but none of the Western powers responded. After all, they had undertaken similar imperialist activities in India, China, the Philippines, and many other Asian and African countries. Therefore, when the Japanese finally colonized Korea in 1910, there was no interference or protest from the West. The United States secretly approved of Japan's actions, because Japan had approved of the U.S. control of the Philippines. When Hirobumi Ito appointed Masatake Terauchi as the first governor of Korea, the Korean kingdom officially ceased to exist.

The Japanese annexation of Korea, which lasted until Japan's defeat in World War II, left deep scars. Japanese officials responded to Korean independence movements with harsh persecution, even torture. The most famous incident, the March First Movement, occurred in 1919. This was a massive, nationwide anti-Japanese demonstration in which over two million Koreans participated. In Japan, too, Koreans were often the target of discrimination. During World War II, over a hundred thousand Koreans were forced to relocate to Japan as laborers (and sometimes as prostitutes for the military fighting abroad). Many such Korean immigrants have continued living in Japan even after Korea's independence, and they continue to face discrimination to this day.

An Jun-geun. The Korean patriot who assassinated Hirobumi Ito in October of 1909.

Japanese General Government Building at Waeseongdae, Korea.

27. Cultural Movements in the Meiji Period

The Meiji Period marked the beginning of modern Japan. The country strove mightily to catch up with the standards of the more technologically and socially advanced Western nations. It invested heavily in the development of new educational, military, governmental, and administrative systems. By the end of the Meiji Period in 1912, Western influence could be seen in every corner of Japan, but particularly in the major cities, in everything from architecture to daily life. At the same time, an array of new cultural movements had also emerged.

This was most evident in literature and the arts. For example, the writers Soseki Natsume, who studied in London, and Ogai Mori, who studied in Germany, and many others penned essays, stories, and novels that incorporated Western literary techniques. Journalism also developed, following Western models. In fact, the Japanese word for newspaper—*shimbun* ("new hearings")—was created in the Meiji Period by Yukichi Fukuzawa, foremost among Japan's modernizers. This was a period in which even the average Japanese was intrigued by Western customs, and Fukuzawa's best-selling books were the authority on that subject. Throughout his life, Fukuzawa made huge contributions to the cause of education through his writings and translations, and eventually by founding Keio University, the first private university in Japan.

Choya Shimbun, an early activist newspaper (1874–93).

Christianity was officially sanctioned in 1873, and many Japanese Christians who had studied in the United States and Europe played important opinion-making roles. Some of them, like Isoo Abe and Sen Katayama, applied their Christian beliefs to socialist causes after seeing the pathetic conditions of poor farmers and workers. Social contradictions showed a direct correlation to the accomplishments of the industrial revolution. The rich minority possessed the power and dominated the poor majority. Socialists and communists vigorously protested and were oppressed by the government in turn.

Soseki Natsume.

With so much Western influence coming into Japan, it was perhaps inevitable that a reaction should set in. In an effort to protect their Japanese identity, many people reacted to Western penetration with resentment and nationalistic sentiments. Such sentiments were often associated with state Shintoism, supported by the Meiji government as part of its plan to unite Japan under the emperor's glory. Nationalist inclinations linking Shintoism with the emperor's divinity eventually played a role in Japan's entry into World War II.

Ogai Mori.

Yukichi Fukuzawa.

28. Taisho Democracy

The Meiji era ended with Emperor Meiji's death in 1912. Because of Japan's many successes, its international status had improved, and Japan had become a major player in world affairs. When Emperor Taisho succeeded to the throne, the Japanese were actually able to enjoy their achievements. The economic damage of World War I was serious, however, and the government's solution was to raise taxes. That decision moved the public to protest and encouraged widespread social movements, including feminism and communism. On the other hand, one of the distinctive features of the Taisho era was its democratic atmosphere. Politically, the movement for parliamentary democracy spread, and in 1925 suffrage was finally granted to all males above the age of twenty-five. Demonstrations and political gatherings were legalized and frequently held, though communism and socialism were banned in 1925.

The generally democratic mood of the Taisho era encouraged cultural activity. Writers like Ryunosuke Akutagawa, Naoya Shiga, and Junichiro Tanizaki created some of the most notable works in modern Japanese literature. Taisho also saw the dawn of mass media. Radio broadcasts started in 1925, and countless magazines and publications were launched.

In international relations, however, Taisho saw the Japanese military becoming more assertive. During World War I, Japan had joined the Allied powers along with England, France, and the United States. While the war was being fought mainly in Europe, Japan took the opportunity to expand its presence in China. The Japanese army occupied the German-controlled Shandong Peninsula and demanded

Old Tokyo Station, opened on December 20, 1914.

that China grant Japan political and military privileges. In China itself, the weakened Qing Dynasty had given way to the Republic of China, and nationalism became a force in combating foreign imperialism. As a matter of course, the Japanese presence in China, gave rise to anti-Japanese sentiment.

It was around the end of Meiji and the beginning of Taisho that Japan began to invest heavily in its military machine, with China in its sights. After Japan defeated Russia in the Russo-Japanese War of 1904-1905, Japan set about expanding its influence westward, particularly to China. This led to the United States becoming Japan's greatest potential enemy. In 1922, at the urging of the United States, Japan, the U.S., England, France, and Italy signed the Washington Treaty to limit naval armaments. These nations also confirmed their own right to expand their interests in the Pacific and China.

"Kurofuneya," by Yumeji Takehisa, a leading figure in the Taisho Romanticism movement.

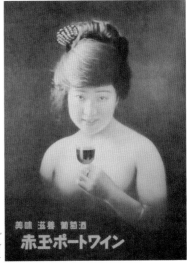

美味 滋養 葡萄酒
赤玉ポートワイン

A poster of "Akadama Port Wine," the first nude advertising poster in 1922.

29. Invasion of Manchuria

When World War I came to an end, the world economy shrank, and Japan faced a serious recession. The efforts of Japanese industry to ride out this recession were nullified by two major catastrophes. In 1923, Tokyo was struck by a major earthquake that killed more than 130,000 people. This disaster destroyed any possibility of quick economic recovery and oppressed the government with a heavy financial burden. Six years later, the famous Wall Street crash of 1929 occurred. Emperor Taisho had passed away in 1926, and Japan was in the fourth year of the reign of Emperor Showa (known outside Japan as Hirohito). The United States had become the world's largest creditor nation in the post-World War I world, so the financial panic was felt in every country, including Japan. The damage was widespread. Not only banks and heavy industries but also agriculture and retailing were severely set back. In rural areas, impoverished farmers sold their daughters; their sons joined the army.

To survive these tumultuous times, Japan's major financial and industrial conglomerates, known as *zaibatsu*, strengthened their ties to government and decided to seek new markets and opportunities in China, particularly Manchuria. *Zaibatsu* such as Mitsui, Mitsubishi, Sumitomo, Yasuda, and, Daiichi had great influence on major political parties and gradually integrated with the military movement.

In 1931, the Japanese army adopted a more aggressive stance in Manchuria and eventually created the puppet state of Manchukuo and installed the dethroned emperor Pu Yi of the Qing Dynasty as emperor. This resulted in Japan being condemned by the international community. Since all the major countries in the League of Nations were opposed to Japanese territorial expansion, the Japanese government decided to withdraw from the League.

World War I carried many lessons for the world's major powers. They had paid a tremendous price to learn that imperialism can cause irreparable damage on a worldwide scale. Japan itself failed to recognize the value of peace and co-existence in the world community. It remained resentful of the United States and other Western nations that had forced the country open in the nineteenth century, and a

↑ *Japanese cavalry entering Mukden (Shenyang).*

← *Emperor Puyi wearing a Manchukuo uniform.*

fanatic nationalism developed. The military, particularly the army, with its arrogant superiority complex, manipulated public opinion, with the support of the right wing. Various social movements were surpressed as unpatriotic.

In 1932, radical junior navy officers assassinated Tsuyoshi Inukai, the prime minister, who headed the Seiyu-kai, the majority party in the Diet. And on February 26, 1936, a group of young military officers, who were opposed to the close relationship between the *zaibatsu* and the government, launched a coup d'etat and killed several Diet members, including Prime Minister Makoto Saito, a former naval officer. Amid the tumult, the military gradually assumed a dominant position in the central government, and the invasion of China took on a more aggressive dimension. In consequence, the democratic gains made in the Taisho era were completely swept away.

After 1923 Great Kanto earthquake, "Japan Relief Movement" was held in Chicago.

30. War Against China

After the Japanese army seized Manchuria, anti-Japanese sentiment spread in China. This sentiment was so strong that a truce was called between the Communists, under Mao Zedong, and the Nationalists, which officially governed China under the leadership of Chiang Kai-shek. The two sides agreed in 1936 to create a united front to resist the Japanese.

To crush this alliance Japan launched a massive attack in 1937, overwhelming a Chinese garrison at Lugou (Marco Polo) Bridge near Beijing. The Japanese occupied Shanghai, Nanjing (the Chinese capital), and many other major cities. It was during this time that the Japanese army committed atrocities in Nanjing, killing several hundred thousand Chinese soldiers and citizens. The Chinese government escaped from Nanjing to Chongqing in Sichuan.

However, long drawn-out battles in the vast Chinese territory stretched the Japanese army thin. They could occupy cities, but it was impossible to keep mountains and rural areas under their control. Also, the Japanese activities created serious tensions with the United States and England, which had considerable interests in China. They officially supported China and established economic sanctions against Japan. In Manchuria, the Japanese army attacked the Soviet Union in Nomonhan in 1939 over a territorial dispute. Stalin's army emerged victorious, and the two countries agreed thereafter to respect the borders of Mongolia and Manchukuo.

By now Japan was isolated from the international community and seen as inimical to movements for international democracy and peace. Japan was also seen as encroaching on Western assets created in Asia over more than three centuries.

Germany and Italy were making similarly aggressive efforts in Europe. When World War II broke out in Europe in 1939, Germany's strength was formidable. Finally, Germany, Italy, and Japan became official allies with a treaty signed in 1940 under the cabinet led by Prime Minister Fumimaro Konoe. Thus, the Axis powers came into being.

In response to the economic sanctions and the necessity of continuing the war against China, Japan proceeded to invade Southeast Asia to maintain stable supplies of oil and other resources. Japanese forces invaded French-controlled Vietnam in 1941, resulting in the U.S. decision to ban oil exports to Japan. England and the Netherlands quickly followed suit.

Domestically, the government continued to manipulate public opinion and call for all Japanese to unite to overcome this national crisis. In 1938, the State General Mobilization Law was passed, enabling government control over all media, industry, and individual citizens to prosecute the war effort. In 1940 all political parties were conflated into one, the Imperial Rule Assistance Association. As a result, the Diet became nothing more than a rubber stamp for government and military decisions. The police, both regular and military, clamped down on anti-government movements and kept a watchful eye on the daily lives of ordinary citizens. In effect, Japan had become a war machine.

Chinese soldiers leaving Beijing under threat of Japanese invasion.

31. The Pacific War and World War II

The extent of Emperor Hirohito's involvement in making the final decision to invade China and wage war against the Allied nations remains a mystery. Japan was clearly under strong military leadership, which manipulated not only the Japanese public but the government and the emperor himself. On the other hand, there were men like Prime Minister Fumimaro Konoe, who wanted to tone down the military's ambitions and find a compromise with the nations embargoing Japan. There were also other high-ranking officials, such as former Prime Minister Mitsumasa Yonai and Admiral Isoroku Yamamoto, who were reluctant to go to war with the Allies.

As the fatal day approached, Japan signed a neutrality pact with the German-besieged Soviet Union in April of 1941 to secure the northern front in Manchuria. Second, the government sent diplomatic delegations to the United States to attempt to ease tensions and economic sanctions. President Roosevelt and his secretary of state, Cordell Hull, demanded full withdrawal of the Japanese army from China. However, even while the negotiations were being conducted, the Japanese army stubbornly ignored directions from the civilian government and expanded its war effort to areas throughout China and Southeast Asia. This increased tensions with the United States and England.

U.S. Navy battleship sinking alongside Ford Island, Pearl Harbor.

Finally, the army general Hideki Tojo became prime minister in October 1941. He decided on a full assault against the United States and England and had the Japanese navy and air force attack Pearl Harbor on December 7, 1941 (December 8 in Japan). The U.S. navy in Hawaii was taken completely by surprise—seven battleships and about half of the aircraft there were destroyed. Simultaneously, Japanese forces attacked Malaysia and Singapore and occupied most of Southeast Asia, including the Philippines, where a U.S. base was located. A number of South Pacific islands were also occupied. Within six months of Pearl Harbor, the Japanese army was making preparations to invade Australia.

Japanese pro-war propaganda was centered on the concept of a Greater East Asia Co-prosperity Sphere. This was intended to mean that Japan would help other Asian nations stand up to and achieve independence from Western imperialism, but it was perceived quite differently outside Japan. Ironically, if Japan had not annexed Korea and invaded China, this propaganda may have received some sympathy—but the reality was far removed from the ideology.

Isoroku Yamamoto.

President Franklin D. Roosevelt.

32. The Atomic Bomb and Surrender

Japan's offensive was successful for the first six months or so. Then the U.S. navy defeated the Japanese navy in the Battle of Midway. This became the turning point in the war. American economic and military power was more substantial than Japan's, and the longer the war continued, the more obvious Japan's weaknesses became.

Starting in the South Pacific, the United States began a counter-offensive, gradually pushing the Japanese back to the north. In China, the Japanese army was depleting its resources in fending off endless guerrilla attacks. In Southeast Asia, England pushed the Japanese back from Burma. After taking Saipan in 1944, the U.S. air force started a bombing campaign on Japan itself and in the Pacific gradually overcame the Japanese navy. In response, the Japanese air force resorted to suicidal *kamikaze* attacks. By April 1945, U.S. forces had begun landing on Okinawa.

In Europe, Italy had surrendered in 1943, and the Allied nations were attacking Germany from both sides. In the same year, Roosevelt, Churchill, and Chiang Kai-shek met in Cairo to discuss postwar arrangements. Stalin and Roosevelt met again in Yalta in February 1945 to confirm that the Soviet Union would invade Manchuria from the north, repudiating the neutrality pact with Japan. After the fall of Nazi Germany, the Allied leaders issued the Potsdam Declaration in July 1945, demanding that Japan surrender unconditionally.

The Potsdam Declaration included the elimination of militarism, the occupation of mainland Japan, and the return of all foreign territories to the appropriate claimants. While Prime Minister Kantaro Suzuki delayed his response, two atomic bombs were dropped—one on Hiroshima on August 6th, the other on Nagasaki on August 9th—killing more than 320,000 innocent civilians. The Soviet Union promptly declared war on Japan and invaded Manchuria.

On August 14th, after prolonged argument and discussion, the government decided to accept the Potsdam Declaration, and Emperor Hirohito made an announcement to the nation over the radio. On September 2nd, the surrender was officially signed on the U.S. battleship Missouri in Tokyo Bay and the Japanese military dismantled.

As a result, Korea became independent, Taiwan was returned to China, and southern Sakhalin reverted to the Soviet Union. Japan had suffered the loss of 3.1 million lives and immeasurable damage to its land and people. Even long after the war, atomic bomb victims in Hiroshima and Nagasaki died from leukemia. In China, countless Japanese children were separated from their parents in the postwar chaos; many were never reunited.

Japan, as the aggressor nation, completely lost the trust of its Asian neighbors. Even now, many Asian countries are quite nervous about the development of the Japanese military. The essential challenge for Japan is to convince them that Japan will continue to reject the use of war as an instrument of national policy, an issue that recently has once again come to the fore.

On the other hand, the United States and England had obligations as winners. Having fought against militarism, they could not very well oppose Asian yearnings for independence from Western influence. The old Western imperialism, which had gained the West large interests and many privileges in China and other Asian nations, began to erode. World War II, particularly the Pacific war, brought an end to imperialism in Asia.

Atomic cloud over Hiroshima.

Foreign Minister Mamoru Shigemitsu signs the Instrument of Surrender.

33. Occupation and Reform

The Occupation of Japan was carried out under the leadership of General Douglas MacArthur, who was appointed Supreme Commander of the Allied Powers (SCAP). SCAP communicated with the Japanese government through General Headquarters (GHQ).

The first task of the Allied Powers was to hold trials to prosecute war criminals. The International Military Tribunal for the Far East was convened in May 1946, and twenty-eight military and political leaders were charged with participating in a joint conspiracy to start and wage war, including former Prime Minister Hideki Tojo, among many others prosecuted for lesser crimes. Similar courts were held both inside and outside Japan, and 920 defendants in all were sentenced to death. The emperor, however, was neither tried nor sent to prison, because SCAP felt he could play an important role in unifying the Japanese public.

Next, SCAP set about making Japan a democratic nation. Over 200,000 bureaucrats who had cooperated in war activities were purged from public office. The old constitution was scrapped and a new one administered in May 1947. Under the new constitution, the emperor was redefined as the symbol of the nation instead of as a divinity. Also, Article IX stated that Japan would never again resort to military force as a means of settling international disputes.

Reflecting democratic ideals, the new constitution provided for parliamentary democracy, including universal suffrage for all eligible citizens, both male and female. Among the many other reforms, basic democratic freedoms such as freedom of speech, assembly, and union activity were ensured. Since the *zaibatsu* were a major factor in the Japanese invasion of Asia, GHQ ordered them dismantled. The agricultural system was also reformed, with tenants now able to own their land.

The war was so devastating that myriads of people were bereft of homes and jobs. Food was in short supply and many urban citizens starved. With union activity and freedom of speech guaranteed, strikes and demonstrations were frequent occurrences, causing SCAP and GHQ to fear the rise of Communism.

In fact, the world political situation was already moving quickly toward the Cold War era, and the United States strongly favored keeping Japan at the strategic forefront of democratic countries in East Asia.

Accordingly, U.S. Occupation policy gradually shifted. While maintaining the goals of making Japan democratic and capitalist, the United States now favored an independent country with the military and economic power to serve as a buffer against the Communist regimes in Russia and China and protect open markets in East Asia.

To achieve that goal, several American specialists were dispatched to help implement changes in the Japanese tax and business systems. At the same time, Japan's rearmament was initiated. The new Japanese military was called the *Jieitai*, or Self-Defense Forces. Whether the Self-Defence Forces are constitutional is still a matter of dispute.

Based on this revised Japan policy, the San Francisco Peace Treaty was concluded in 1951 with forty-two allied nations. Simultaneously, the U.S.–Japan Mutual Security Treaty, was signed, with Japan approving U.S. military presence on its soil. In 1956 Japan applied to join the United Nations and was approved.

Thus, the Occupation officially ended, except for Okinawa and the Ogasawara Islands. In Okinawa, where most of the U.S. military bases are located, there have been occasional protests against the American presence as an obstacle to achieving a full peace and fulfilling local needs. The Ogasawara chain was returned to Japan in 1968, and Okinawa's occupation status ended in 1971 when it reverted to Japanese control. The postwar era had finally come to an end.

Emperor Hirohito and General MacArthur.

34. Era of High Economic Growth and the Bubble Economy

Devastated by World War II, Japan needed strong leadership to get back on its feet. Initially, MacArthur filled that need. However, it was the Japanese government and bureaucracy who eventually galvanized the economy and drove it forward. Since the Meiji Restoration in 1868, bureaucrats had always been the real power holders in the Japanese government.

Japan's economic recovery, triggered initially by the Korean War (1950–53), gained speed in the 1960s. After Prime Minister Hayato Ikeda promised that Japanese income would double within a decade, the economy took off like a rocket and the annual GDP growth rate exceeded 10%. Per capita income actually tripled in the 1960s. The symbolic events representing this amazing economic recovery were the Tokyo Olympic Games in 1964—the first Olympics held in Asia—and the inauguration in the same year of the Shinkansen, the famous Bullet Train.

But this rapid growth exacted a price, with escalating pollution and vast increases in the cost of goods and real estate. The standard of living simply could not keep pace. Improvement in housing standards remains one of Japan's most serious problems, particularly in big cities.

Economic success gradually restored Japanese confidence, and by the 1970s renewed Japan became increasingly involved in international affairs. In the 1980s Japan became the world's number two economic power and number one in foreign aid. On the debit side, key Western trading partners frequently accused Japan of enjoying a trade surplus because of unfair trading practices.

Now, after years of economic success, it is questionable whether Japan still needs such a strongly entrenched bureaucracy. On the issue of trade regulations, regulations were necessary to steer the Japanese economy through the devastation following the war. However, once the world entered the era of market globalization, many of the old regulations became outdated. But bureaucrats have resisted policy change, because that would mean a reduction of their power and prestige. In the meanwhile, both domestic and international pressure for deregulation has intensified.

In fact, Japan has been urged to share the responsibility of being a global partner. This has been a hot item of public discussion in Japan. Since the time of Prime Minister Yasuhiro Nakasone (served 1982–87), one of the most important public issues has been whether Japan should give any kind of military

Tokyo Olympics 1964 Opening Ceremony.

aid to the U.N. peace-keeping forces in the world's unstable areas. In a partial resolution to this issue, in 1992 the Diet passed a law that permitted the Self-Defense Forces to participate in U.N. medical, refugee repatriation, logistical support, infrastructural reconstruction, election-monitoring, and policing operations under strictly limited conditions. Further expansion of the role of the Self-Defence Forces is now under consideration by the Shinzo Abe administration.

By the late 1980s, the strong growth of the Japanese economy spawned the term "bubble economy." The value of real estate escalated precipitously; financial institutions benefitted hugely and encouraged industry to wider investment; Japanese businesses expanded their offices and factories worldwide.

Unfortunately, economic inflation led to corruption and fostered feelings of distrust toward politicians and bureaucrats. When the bubble burst in 1991 owing to the devaluation of real estate, the economy slid into a recession that lasted throughout the 1990s. The public's approval rating of the government and bureaucracy went downhill along with the economy.

With the return to power of the Liberal Democratic Party's Shinzo Abe as prime minister in 2012, an attempt is being made to defeat deflation and reinvigorate the Japanese economy through increased government spending and unprecedented money easing. The long-term results of this effort are yet to be seen.

35. Japan and the World in the Twenty-First Century

In the twenty-first century, the use of the term "postwar" is fading fast. The generation that experienced World War II is disappearing. Between the Meiji period and the war, Japan's policy of "Enrich the nation, strengthen the armed forces" led to various contradictions, such as colonial expansion while criticizing Western and some Asian countries interference, increasing militarism while advocating peace and harmony, and pursuing Westernization while remaining highly traditional in many aspects. It was during the postwar period that these also began to fade away or to be examined critically.

These same issues, however, are not unrelated to the tense global situation today. The September 2001 terrorist attacks in the United States triggered turmoil and warfare throughout the Muslim world from Central Asia to North Africa. Japan's leader at the time, Prime Minister Junichiro Koizumi, advocated structural reform of the political and business world in Japan and supported the United States' Middle East policy, strengthening the alliance between the two nations.

Since then, the world has been hit by various upheavals, such as Russia's invasion of Ukraine and Israel's attack on the Gaza Strip in 2023, causing tremendous tension everywhere. As the economic impact of these wars has spread, the anxiety they brought has had a considerable impact on public opinion among the Japanese people.

For one thing, the complex and rapidly evolving global situation has sparked vigorous debates about how Japan should respond. In particular, the question of whether Japan should expand its defensive capabilities or even amend the Constitution to formally establish a military force is an extremely divisive issue.

Of course, the debates are not just limited to places like the Middle East. In the twenty-first century, North Korea has developed nuclear missiles and repeatedly acted in a threatening manner toward Japan. Furthermore, in the 2000s, several large-scale anti-Japanese movements in China have promoted nationalism in China itself, causing great concern among the Japanese public.

Subsequently, the national reform movement inaugurated by President Xi Jinping in 2013 led to increased tensions between China and the United States. China has threatened the East China Sea, the South China Sea, and even the continued existence of Taiwan. This has led to a sense of crisis in Japan. Japan's economy has been in a prolonged slump since the 1990s, and the additional threats from its neighbors have contributed to a growing sense of uncertainty and apprehension.

The educational system and the structure of public-private economic activities, which were driven by the state and agreed upon by many citizens to promote postwar reconstruction and growth, are often criticized as being obsolete these days. Furthermore, as the lifestyles of young people have changed, there has been a noticeable shift in public attitudes about lifestyles and work.

Individuals' needs have become more valued, and awareness of gender equality in the workplace has grown. The traditional lifetime employment system has also been shaken by both the changing nature of the modern economy and people's increased emphasis on personal happiness rather than work and the good of the company.

Unfortunately, reforms to address education and workplace issues while taking into account shifts in people's fundamental values have not made sufficient progress. In addition, business and technological innovation, which in the past were carried out with great enthusiasm, seem to be fading.

As a result, Japan, which once a dominant force in the world economically due to its remarkable manufacturing sector, has been overtaken by other countries in various fields, especially those in which IT plays a significant role. Japan has repeatedly tried to implement reforms to cope with these changes, but enormous challenges remain.

In 2010, the rapidly growing Chinese economy surpassed Japan in terms of GDP. Since that time, China has become the biggest threat to Japan, both militarily and in business. In addition, the fact that Japan has been unable to improve relations with its former colony Korea has made it difficult to strengthen ties with the rising economic powerhouse and is a contributing factor in Japan's troubles internationally. Japan clearly needs to strengthen its relations with other Asian nations.

36. Japan's Challenges

In March 2011, a giant earthquake and tsunami struck Japan. The Fukushima Daiichi nuclear power plant experienced a partial meltdown, and concerns about environmental pollution related to the disposal of nuclear waste spread around the world. Japan was already suffering from a sluggish economy and poor relations with its neighbors. The disaster raised even more questions about Japan's crisis management and leadership.

After the earthquake, the Democratic Party of Japan, which had been in power for many years, suffered a crushing defeat. Subsequently, major earthquakes occurred in Kumamoto in Kyushu in 2016 and on the Noto Peninsula in central Japan in 2024.

Prime Minister Shinzo Abe strongly promoted efforts to bring about a national revival with the slogan "Beautiful Japan." Beginning with his reelection in 2012, Abe began pushing for large-scale economic reforms to ensure that Japan would continue to grow. He remained in power until 2020.

As these policies were promoted, however, issues such as educational problems, wealth gaps, and economic disparities between urban and rural areas that had existed since the bursting of Japan's economic bubble became issues of greater concern. Addressing climate change due to global warming and other factors has also emerged as a major issue for the nation. Another major challenge has been that the strong leadership of the central government promoted centralized policies for the country as a whole while policies that made the most of the uniqueness of local regions seemed to be taking a backseat.

Unfortunately, despite the Abe administration's vision, issues such as the promotion of equal opportunities for women and the struggles of single-parent households have not been fully resolved to date. It is also alarming that the basic conditions for Japan to be globally competitive in the age of AI and IT have not been resolved. Without better English proficiency, an emphasis on IT in the business world, and the fostering of a globally-minded workforce, Japan will face tremendous difficulties in the coming years.

Nevertheless, Japan is still a nation that maintains the economic strength and human resources to lead the world. The challenges described here are not unique to Japan, but are common to many countries around the world.

The question is whether Japan, now that it seems to have emerged from the postwar period, can continue to play a leadership role by promoting economic, cultural, and human exchange with South Korea, China, and other Southeast Asian countries. This will require a change in the national mindset, which has often diverged from that of the rest of Asia. Japan may need to position itself as a country that can interact with the Western world while sharing Asian values and make bold educational and economic reforms commensurate with this stance for the future.

Appearance of Fukushima Daiichi Nuclear Power Plant Unit 3 after the explosion.

A house destroyed by 2016 Kumamoto earthquake.

37. Toward the Future

There are two main problems that Japan must solve. First and foremost is the reduction of the national budget deficit that has accumulated during the long economic slump since the 1990s. With the savings rate of the Japanese people decreasing year by year, the quality of public services and effective exchanges with foreign countries will suffer if this issue is not resolved.

Inseparable from this problem is the second issue, the country's declining birthrate. It is predicted that Japan's population will decline by more than 40% by 2090. This means that Japan will be at the same population level as it was in the early Meiji period, and a small, young population will have to support a large, aging population. The declining birthrate will have a major impact not only on tax revenues but also on policy management itself.

Difficult decisions are going to have to be made about whether or not to cut government spending, how the pension system will be able to operate in the future, whether to allow immigrants in to replace retired workers, and a host of other extremely difficult-to-solve problems.

It is also urgent that Japan solve the problem of taking care of the elderly and find a way to reintegrate them into the labor force, as well as dealing with the gender disparity issue.

At a time when the country has been trying to overcome such challenges, a major fundraising scandal erupted in the governing party in 2023. It is very unfortunate that because of this incident and others like it, the public has become extremely distrustful of politics.

It is also worrisome to observe a growing sense of suspicion toward the bureaucracy and even local administrations, as there are many challenges that both the people and politics must overcome in order to demonstrate strong leadership and win the trust of the world.

In addition, the spread of the coronavirus, which closed off most of the world's human interaction between 2020 and the spring of 2023, seems to have put the brakes on solutions to Japan's revitalization challenges. On the other hand, the changes in lifestyle caused by the pandemic have also had the effect of shifting the balance between industry and labor by placing more emphasis on individuals' needs. The pandemic has also been a catalyst for future industries, such as logistics, to have a greater impact on society and encouraged remote work and conducting business online.

Despite the negative legacy of the coronavirus, the pandemic has helped to instill new values in people, such as causing them to reevaluate their priorities in terms of lifestyle and work-life balance and encouraging a new appreciation of health and personal relationships.

Economically, Japan used to be a country with numerous cutting-edge companies supplying semiconductors to the world. However, it has rapidly lost market share to companies in fast-growing Asian countries, Europe, and the United States.

Symbolic of this is that TSMC, Taiwan's largest semiconductor manufacturer, is entering Japan. TSMC is a company that has grown rapidly in recent years and is responsible for 50 to 60% of the world's semiconductor market share.

However, Japan still supplies manufacturing equipment and precision instruments to TSMC and other companies. When considering Japan's strengths, it is necessary not only to be aware of them as Japan's own, but also to take a new perspective on how they relate to the world's advanced industries and the future shift to AI, as seen in the automotive industry, etc.

This is partly because the world is becoming more accessible through advances in IT and AI, and partly because a shrinking population could increase Japan's reliance on people and technologies from other countries.

The island nation of Japan has been thrown into a world where it is impossible to argue that it is unique or immune to the forces that affect other societies and economies.

Many years have passed since the time when Japan could singlehandedly determine its own future. Japan's fate in the years to come depends on the future of education, international relations, its leadership, and the consciousness of the Japanese people themselves.

Time Line

12,000 B.C. Jomon Period

Jomon culture / Jomon pottery

300 B.C. Yayoi Period

Yayoi culture / irrigated rice cultivation

A.D. 57 — The Na state of Wa (Japan) sends envoy to the Later Han

239 — Himiko of the Yamatai kingdom sends envoy to the Wei Dynasty

A.D. 300 Yamato Period

ca. 350 — Yamato dynasty established

538 — Arrival of Buddhism

587 — Soga Clan defeats Mononobe Clan

593 — Prince Shotoku becomes regent to Empress Suiko

604 — Seventeen-article constitution promulgated

645 — Taika Reform

701 — Taiho Constitution

710 Nara Period

710 — Imperial court moves to Nara (Heijo)

712 — Kojiki (Records of Ancient Matters)

720 — Nihonshoki (The Chronicles of Japan)

ca. 759 — Man'yoshu (Collection of Myriad Leaves)

784 — Imperial court moves to Nagaoka

794 Heian Period

794 — Imperial court moves to Heian

800- — Tang culture widely adopted

Saicho and Kukai return from China and found two new Buddhist sects

Hiragana and katakana created

ca. 1008 — The Tale of Genji

1016 — Fujiwara clan at the height of its power

1156 — Hogen War

1159-85 — Gempei War

1167 — Taira no Kiyomori appointed grand minister

1185 — Fall of the Heike

1185 Kamakura Period

1192 — Minamoto no Yoritomo appointed shogun

1221 — New Pure Land Buddhist sects established

1274 — First Mongol invasion (Battle of Bun'ei)

1281 — Second Mongol invasion (Battle of Koan)

1333 Muromachi (Ashikaga) Period

1333	Fall of the Kamakura shogunate
1334	Kemmu Restoration
1336	Emperor Godaigo reigns at the court of Yoshino
	Era of Northern and Southern Courts begins
1338	Ashikaga Takauji appointed shogun
1368	Ashikaga Yoshimitsu becomes third shogun
1392	Yoshimitsu consolidates the shogunate
1467-77	Onin War (beginning of Warring States Period)
1543	Portuguese ship makes landfall on Tanegashima
1549	Christianity introduced to Japan by Jesuit missionary Francis Xavier

1568 Azuchi-Momoyama Period

1568	Oda Nobunaga enters Kyoto
1573	End of Muromachi (Ashikaga) shogunate
1582	Honno-ji Incident (death of Oda Nobunaga)
1590	Toyotomi Hideyoshi completes unification of the country
1592	Hideyoshi's first invasion of Korea (Bunroku no eki)
1597	Hideyoshi's second invasion of Korea (Keicho no eki)

1600 Edo Period

1600	Battle of Sekigahara
1603	Tokugawa Ieyasu establishes Tokugawa shogunate
1615	Fall of Toyotomi clan
1637	Shimabara Rebellion
1641	The shogunate completes seclusion policy
1688-	The Genroku era
	Bunraku puppet theater and haiku flourish
1782-	Great Tenmei Famine
1804-	The Bunka-Bunsei era
	Ukiyo-e and Kabuki flourish
1832-	Great Tempo Famine
1853	Commodore Matthew Perry arrives in Uraga Bay
1854	The Treaty of Kanagawa. The end of Japan's isolation policy
1867	Tokugawa Yoshinobu, the last shogun, resigns

1868 Meiji Period

1868	Meiji Restoration
	Boshin War
1877	Seinan War

1885	Cabinet system adopted with Hirobumi Ito as the first prime minister
1894	First Sino-Japanese War
1895	Peace Treaty of Shimonoseki
1902	Anglo-Japanese Alliance
1904	Russo-Japanese War
1905	Peace Treaty of Portsmouth
1910	Japan annexes Korea

1912 Taisho Period

1912	Death of Emperor Meiji
1914	World War I
1919	March First Movement
1922	Washington Naval Treaty
	Magazine/book publication flourishes
	Suffrage granted to all males above 25
	Radio broadcasting begins

1926 Showa Period

1926	Death of Emperor Taisho
1929	Wall Street Crash
1931	Manchurian (Mukden) Incident
1932	Puppet state of Manchukuo established
1936	February 26 Incident
1937	Marco Polo (Lugou) Bridge Incident, setting off second Sino-Japanese War
1939	Nomonhan (Khalkhin Gol) Incident
1940	Tripartite Pact among Japan, Germany, and Italy
1941	Pacific War starts with Japan's attack on Pearl Harbor
1945	United States drops atomic bombs on Hiroshima and Nagasaki. Japan surrenders
1947	New Japanese constitution promulgated
1951	San Francisco Peace Treaty signed
1954	The Lucky Dragon No. 5 is contaminated by a hydrogen bomb test at Bikini Atoll
1955	Liberal Democratic Party formed
	Japan Self-Defense Forces established
1960	Japan-US Security Treaty revised
1964	Olympic Games held in Tokyo
	Tokaido Shinkansen opens
1968	Student movements become active
	Yukio Mishima commits suicide by ritual disembowelment

1970	Osaka Expo held
1971	Nixon Shock
	Yen devalued
1973	First Oil Shock
1979	Second Oil Shock
1985	Plaza Accord
1987	Japanese National Railways privatized

1989 Heisei Period

1989	Death of Emperor Showa
1990s	Economic bubble bursts
1995	Great Hanshin Earthquake
	Tokyo subway sarin gas attack
2001	September 11 terrorist attacks on the U.S.
2002	FIFA World Cup co-hosted by Japan and South Korea
2003	Iraq War begins
2007	Apple releases the iPhone
2008	The collapse of Lehman Brothers triggers a global financial crisis
2009	The Democratic Party of Japan (DPJ) forms the first non-LDP government in 55 years
2011	2011 Tohoku Earthquake and Tsunami
2012	Shinzo Abe becomes Prime Minister and implements "Abenomics," a set of economic policies
2013	Mt. Fuji is registered as a cultural site of world heritage
2016	U.S. President Obama visits Hiroshima
2017	Donald Trump is inaugurated as U.S. president
2018	First U.S.-North Korea summit between Donald Trump and Kim Jong-un

2019 Reiwa Period

2019	Emperor Akihito abdicates the throne, and Crown Prince Naruhito ascends to the throne
2020	COVID-19 pandemic causes cancellation and postponement of various events around the world
2021	Tokyo Olympics held after one-year postponement due to COVID-19
2022	Russian invasion of Ukraine
	Assassination of former Prime Minister Shinzo Abe

Index

Coen Nishiumi

A business consultant and a travel writer, Coen Nishiumi is a frequent magazine contributor on world culture and history. Among his book publications are biographies of Sakamoto Ryoma, Oda Nobunaga, and Soichiro Honda. He is currently based in New York and travels widely as an intercultural business consultant.

JAPAN: A Short History
New Edition

2015年3月7日 　　　初版第1刷発行
2024年4月6日　増補改訂版第1刷発行
2024年7月11日　　　　第2刷発行

著　　　者　西海コエン

監 修 者　ジョン・ギレスピー

リ ラ イ ト　マイケル・ブレーズ

発 行 者　賀川　洋

発 行 所　IBCパブリッシング株式会社
　　　　　〒162-0804
　　　　　東京都新宿区中里町29番3号
　　　　　菱秀神楽坂ビル
　　　　　TEL 03-3513-4511
　　　　　FAX 03-3513-4512
　　　　　www.ibcpub.co.jp

印 刷 所　株式会社シナノパブリッシングプレス

ISBN 978-4-7946-0808-6

Printed in Japan

Front cover: Matsumoto Castle (Nagano Prefecture)
Back cover: Mt. Fuji and the five-story pagoda (Yamanashi Prefecture)
Page 1: Otorii (Grand Gate) of Itsukushima Shrine (Hiroshima Prefecture)

On Japan titles by IBC Publishing

JAPAN: a pictorial portrait
日本写真紀行
ISBN 978-4-7946-0172-8

Soul of Japan: The Visible Essence
日本人のこころ
ISBN 978-4-7946-0135-3

MADE IN JAPAN
日本の匠：世界に誇る日本の伝統工芸
ISBN 978-4-7946-0560-3

MADE IN KYOTO
京都の匠：世界を変える京都の伝統工芸
ISBN 978-4-7946-0626-6

BEAUTIFUL JAPAN
日本人の原風景
ISBN 978-4-7946-0283-1

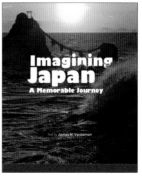

**Imagining Japan:
A Memorable Journey**
ISBN 978-4-7946-0346-3

On Japan titles by IBC Publishing

SAKURA: The Japanese Soul Flower
桜
ISBN 978-4-7946-0262-6

THE BEAUTY OF AUTUMN IN JAPAN
紅葉
ISBN 978-4-7946-0301-2

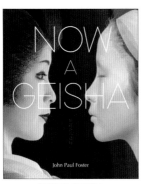

NOW A GEISHA
舞妓から芸妓へ
ISBN 978-4-7946-0512-2

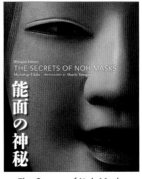

The Secrets of Noh Masks
能面の神秘
ISBN 978-4-7946-0356-2

JAPAN: POETRY AND PLACES
百歌百景
ISBN 978-4-7946-0725-6

TOKYO: Traditions from Islands to Mountains
東京百景
ISBN 978-4-7946-0572-6